DRIVE FAST DON'T STOP

「 WWW.DRIVEFASTDONTSTOP.COM 」

BOOK 19

WEKFEST - JANUARY 2024

♥

WEKFEST

WEKFEST

WEKFEST

WEKFEST

WEKFEST

WEKFEST

WEKFEST

WEKFEST

WEKFEST

WEKFEST

WEKFEST

WEKFEST

CAR SHOW

CAR SHOW

CAR SHOW

CAR SHOW

CAR SHOW

CAR SHOW

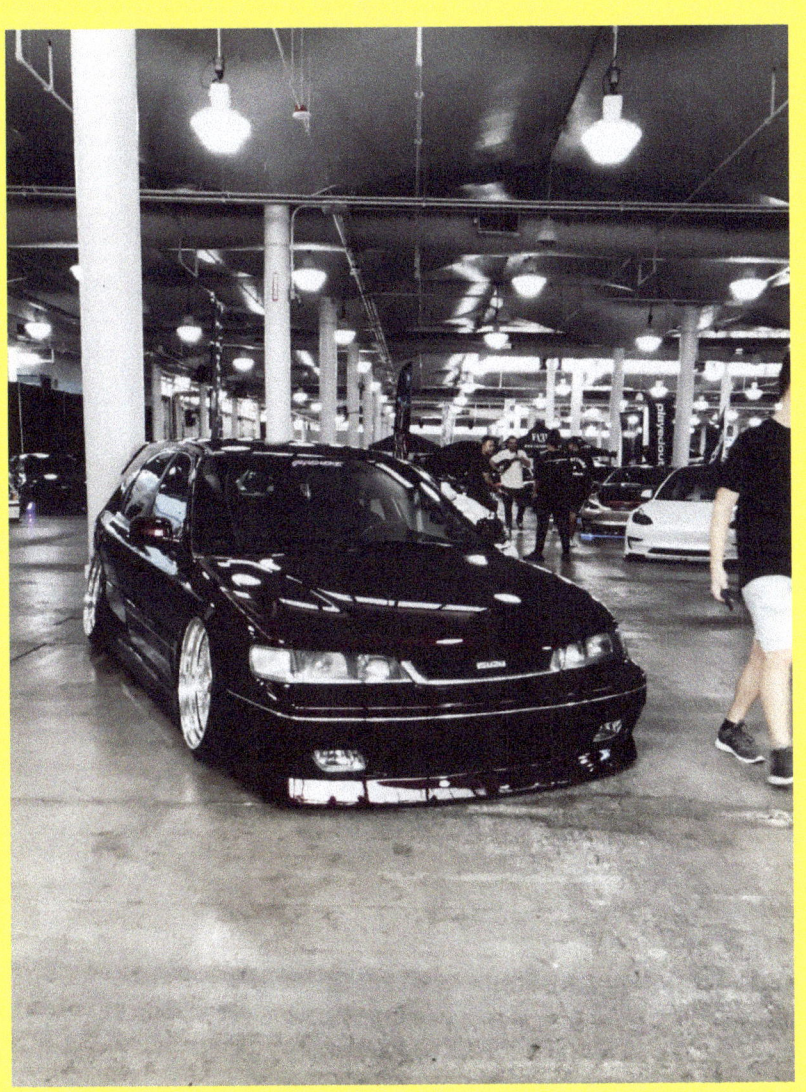

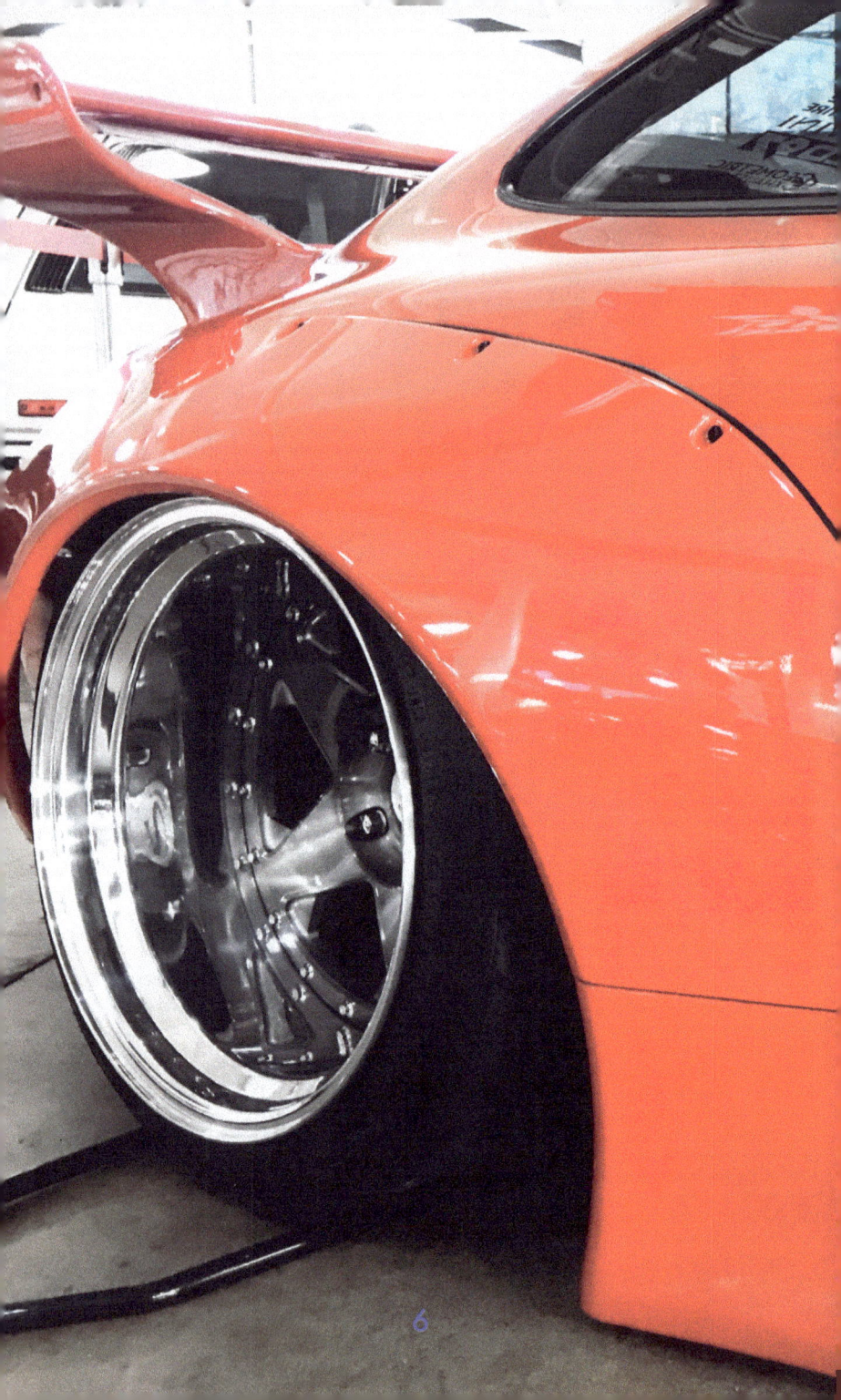

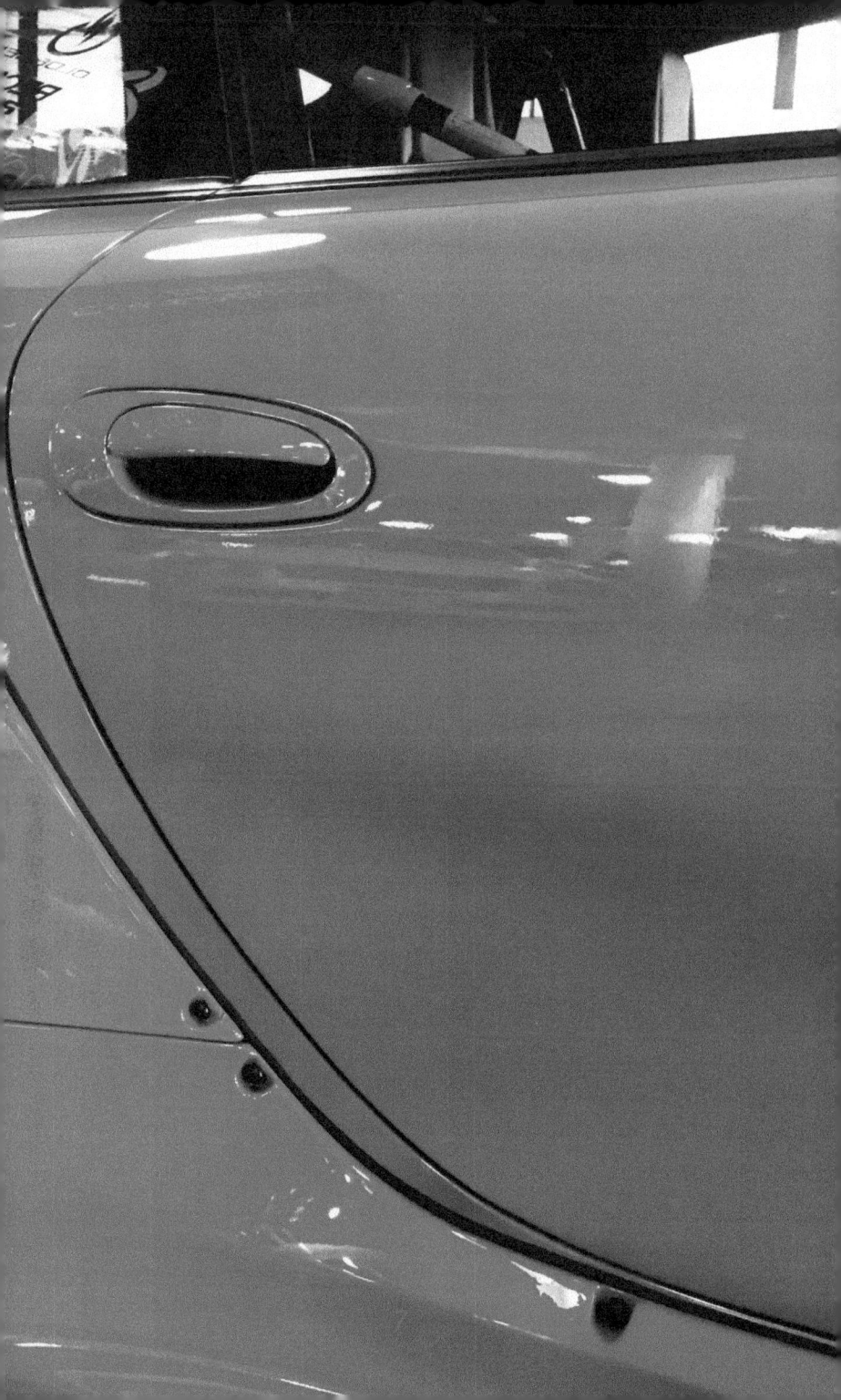

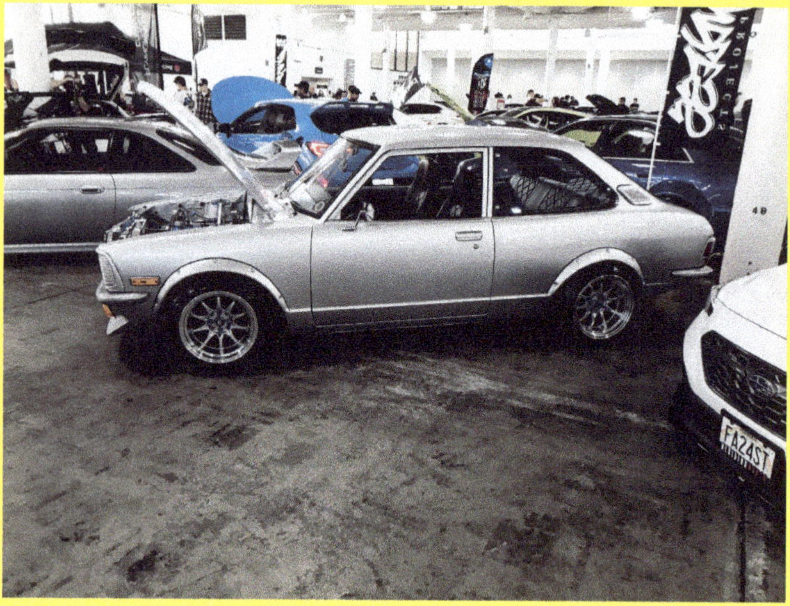

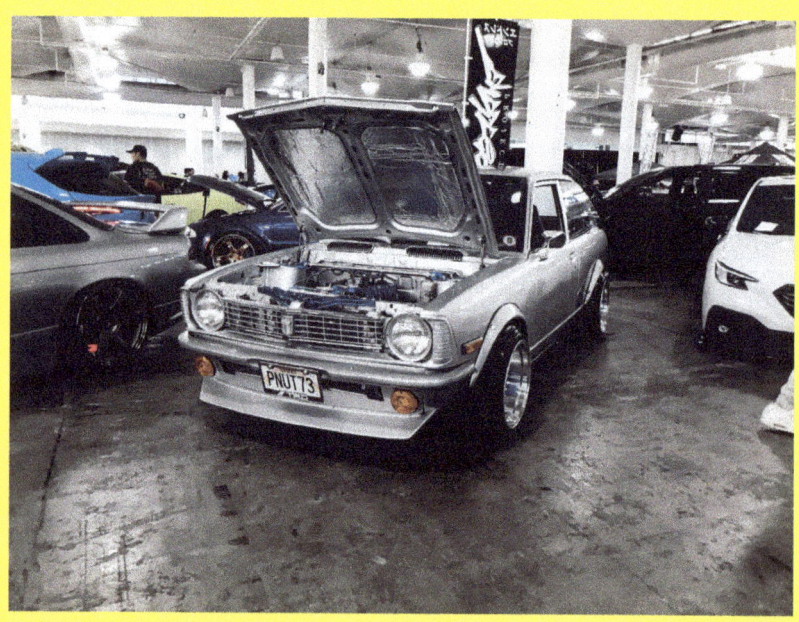

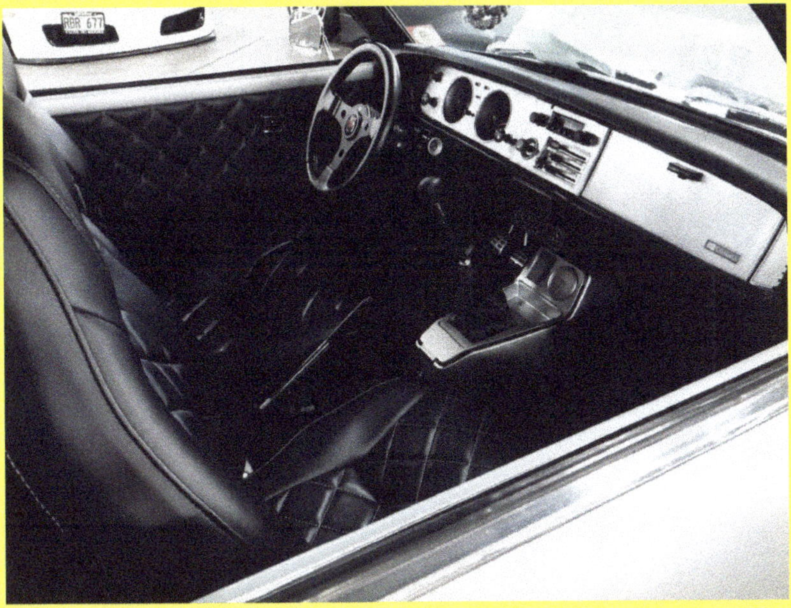
RBR 677

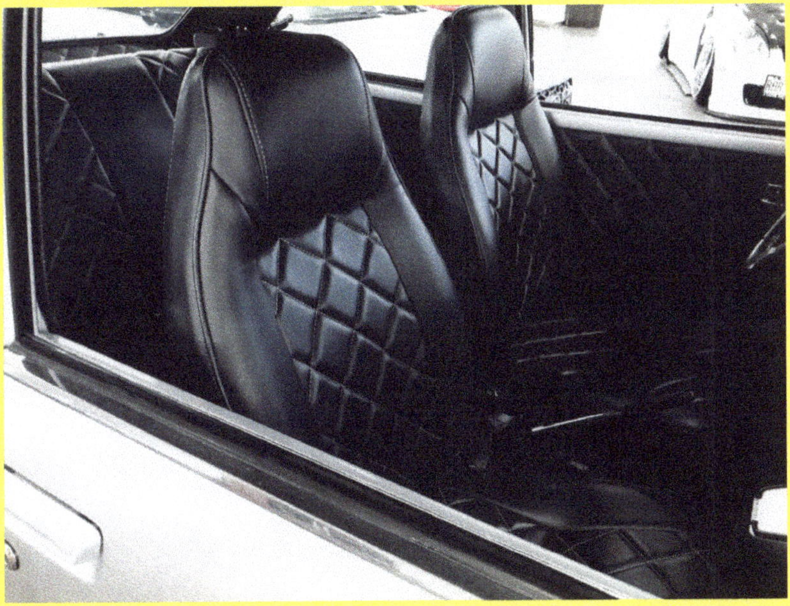

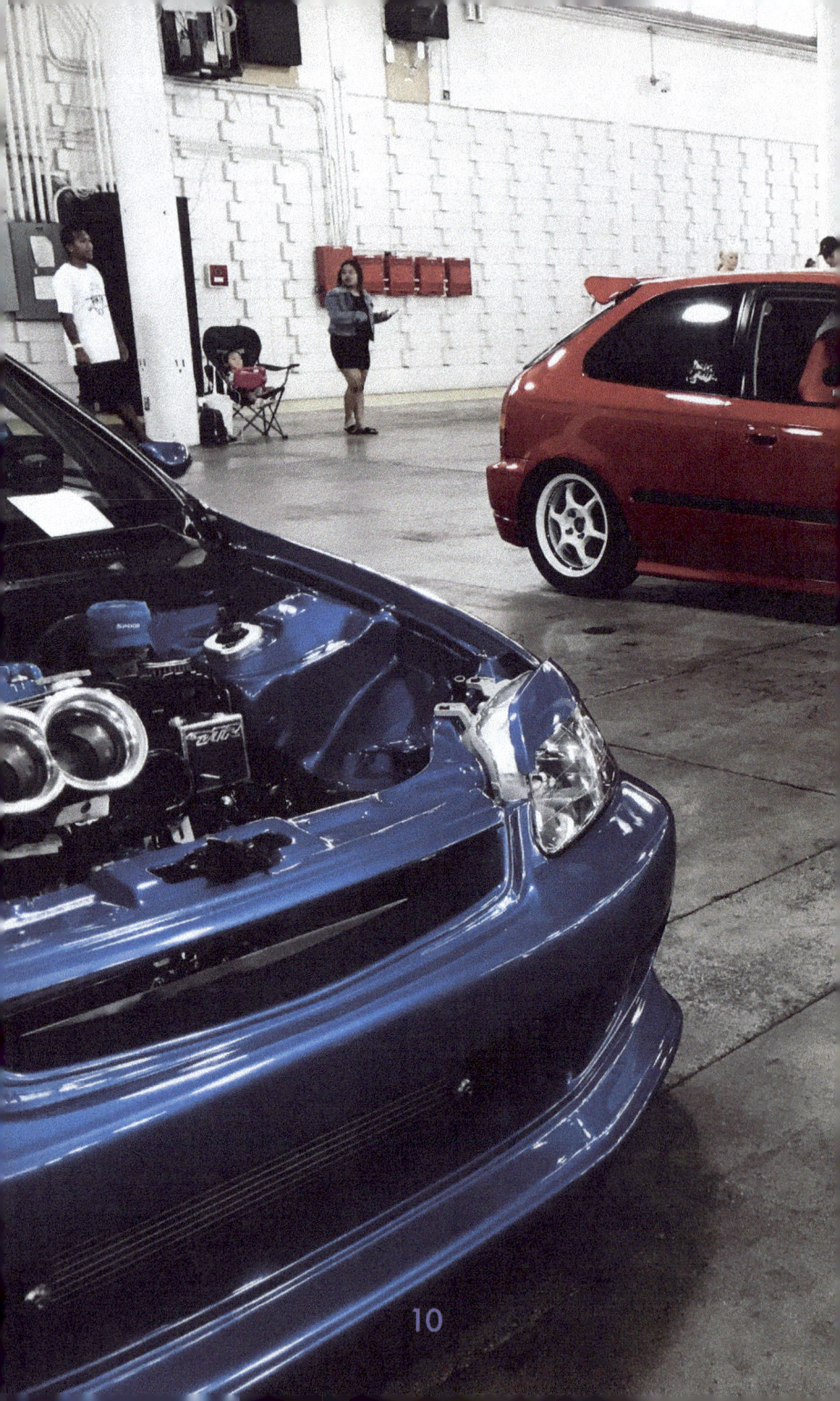

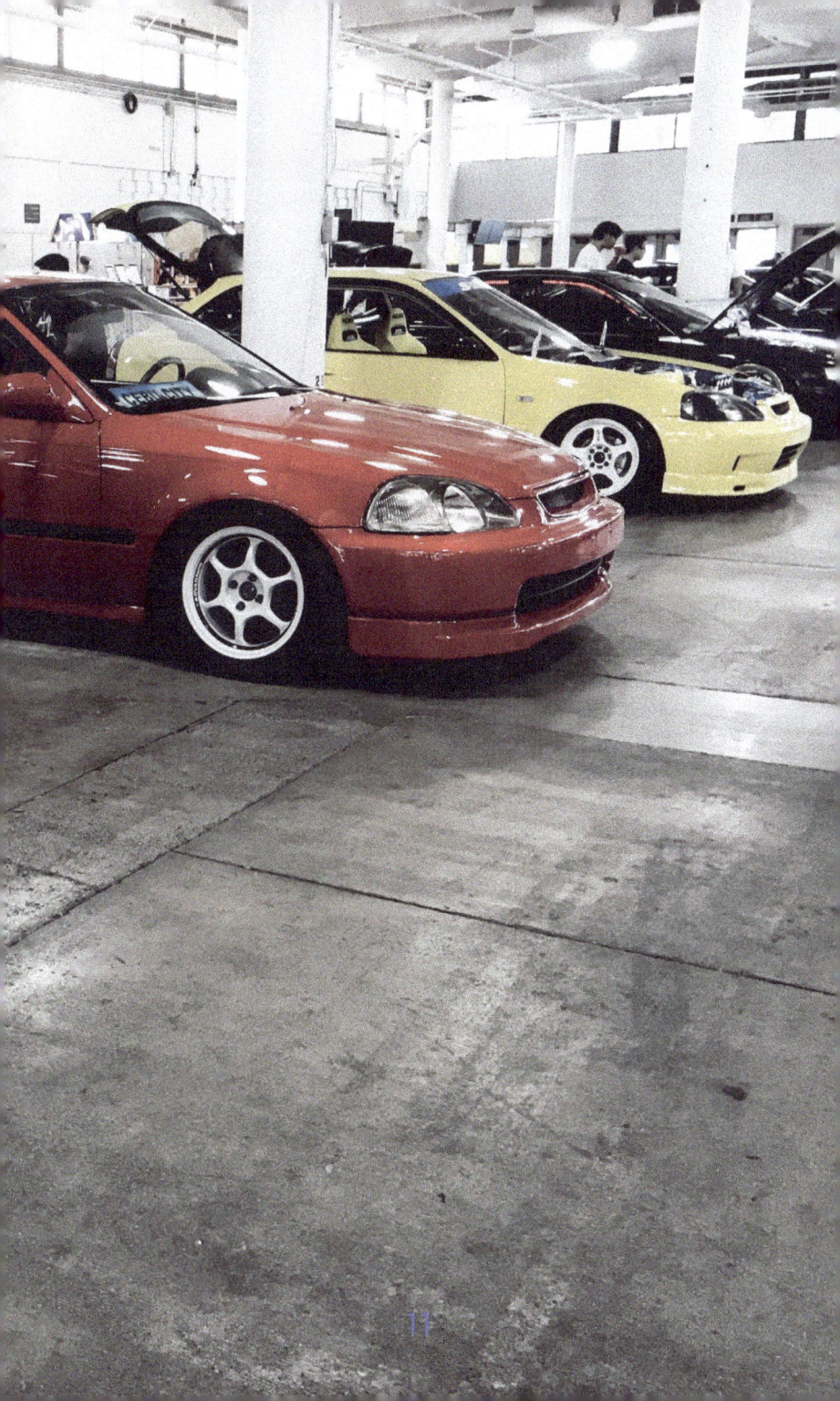

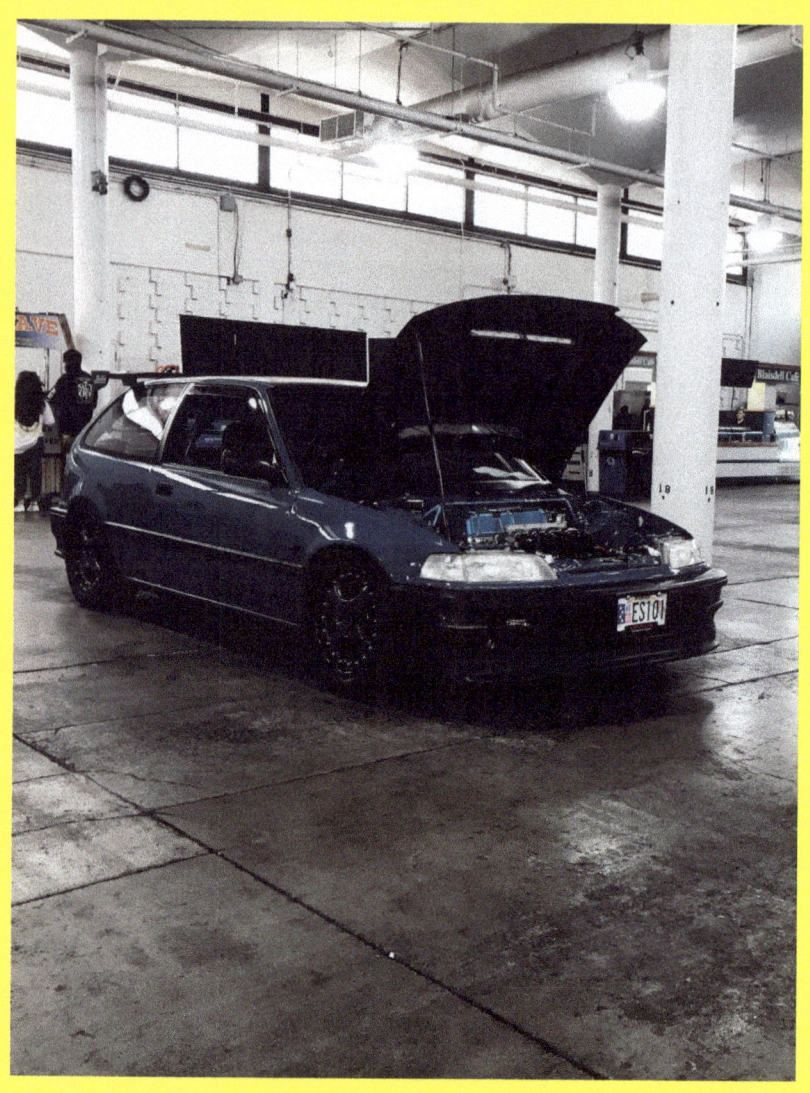

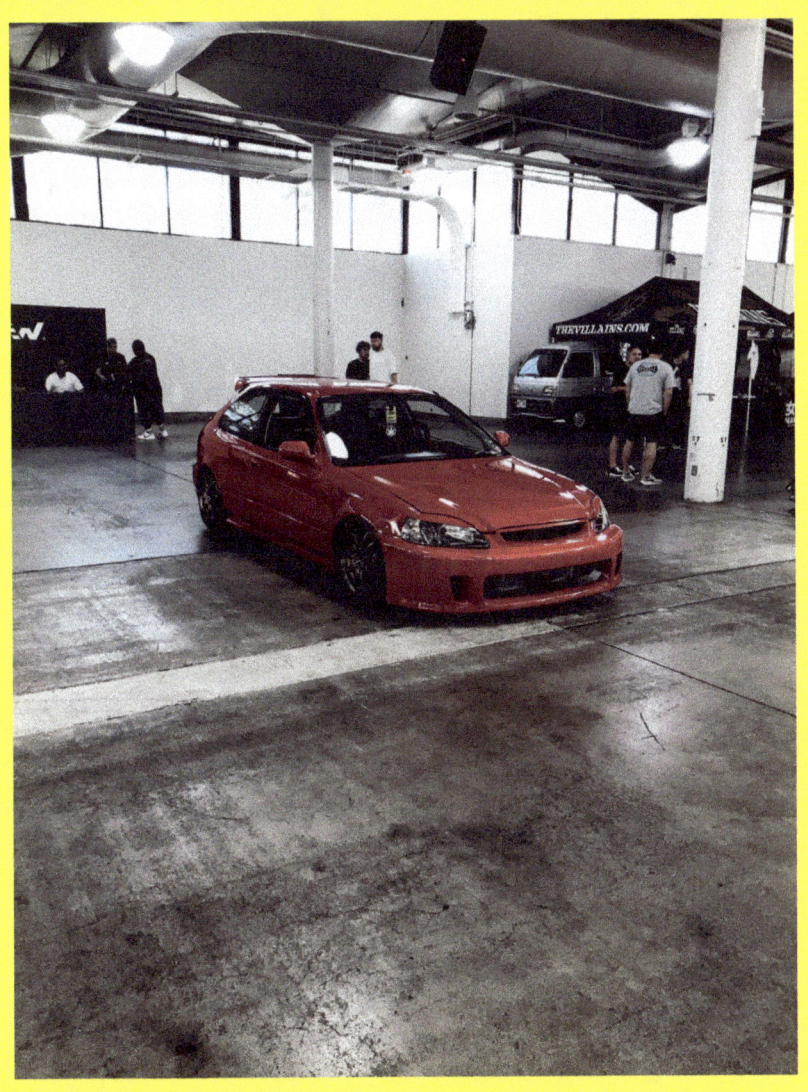

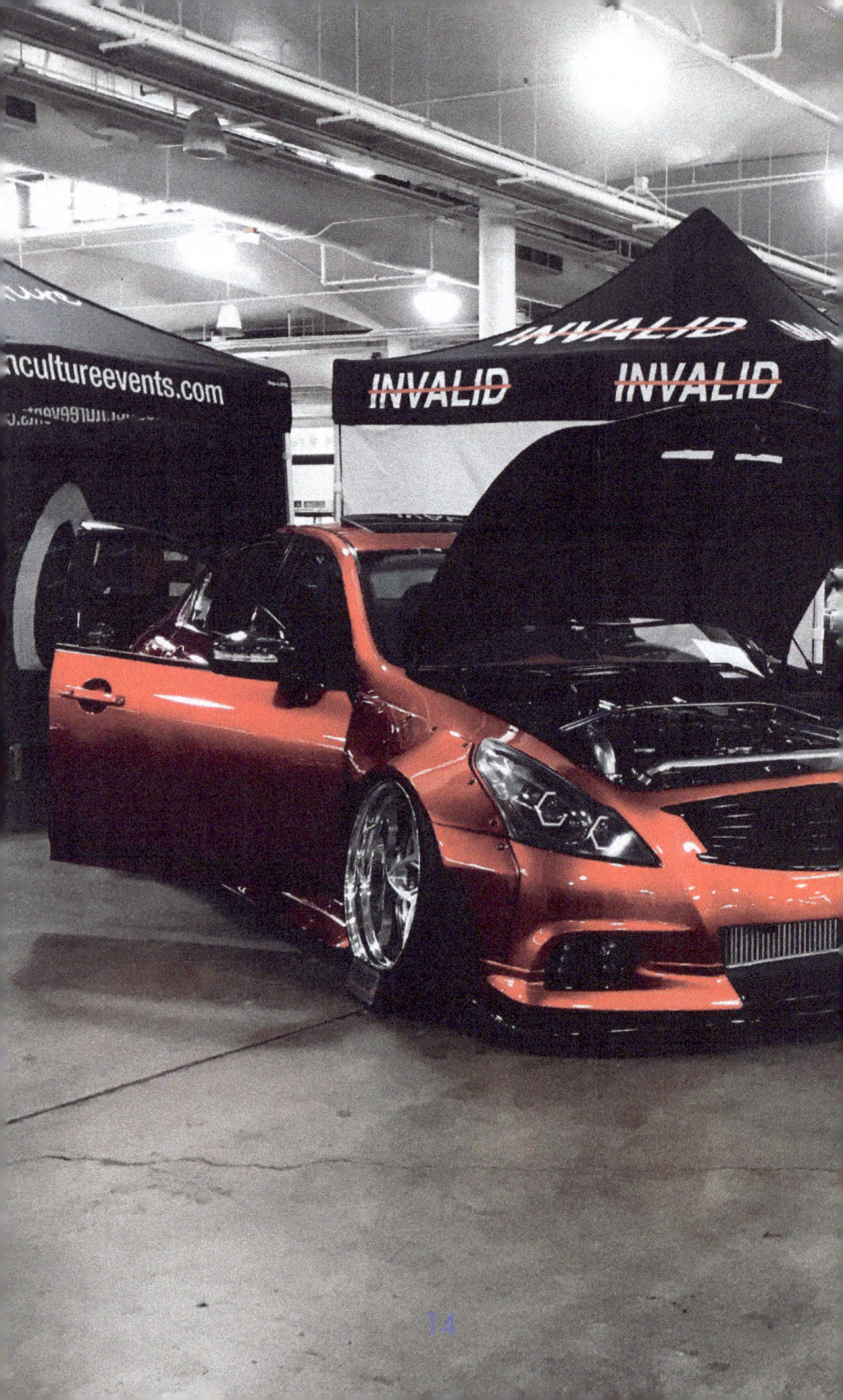

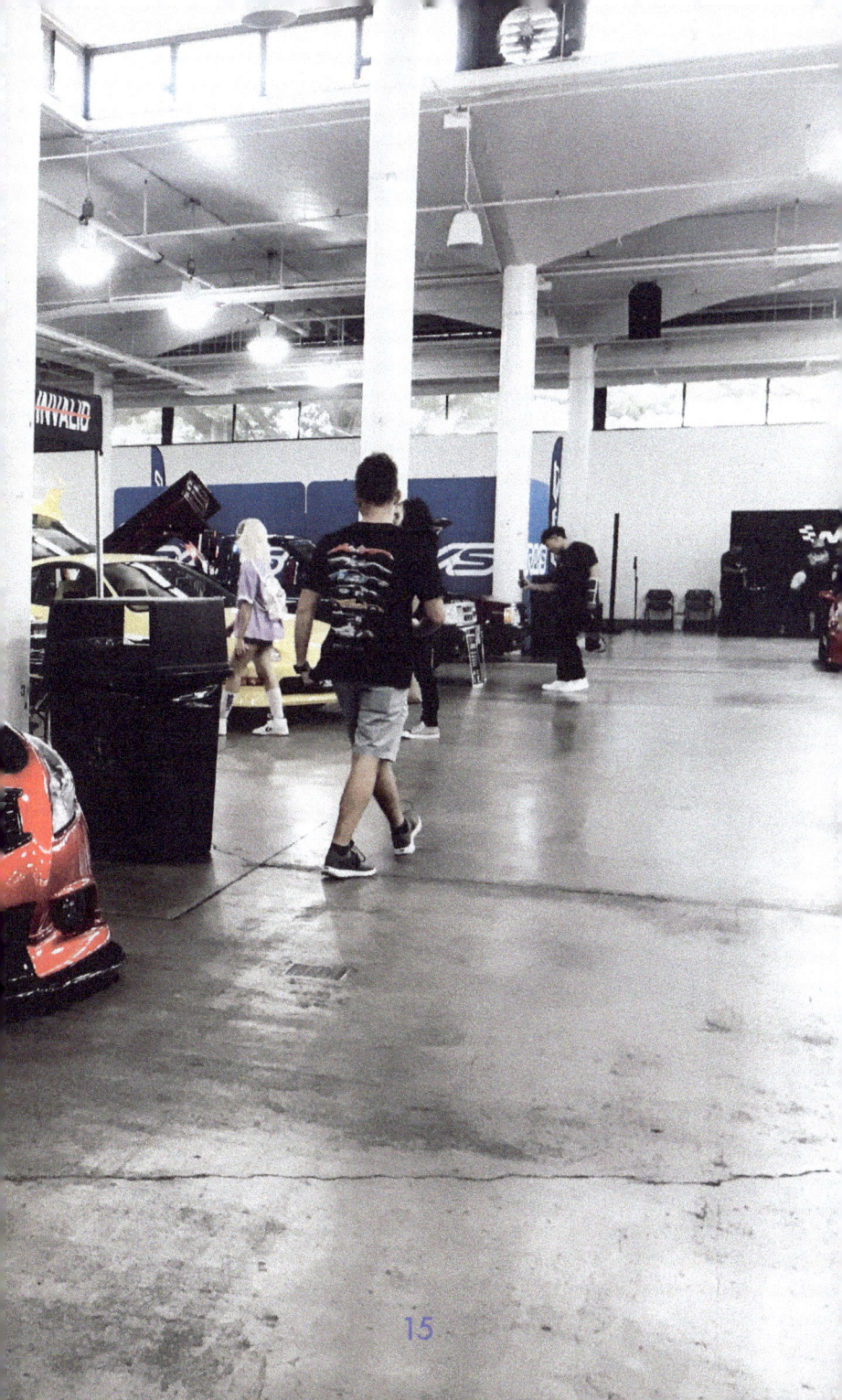

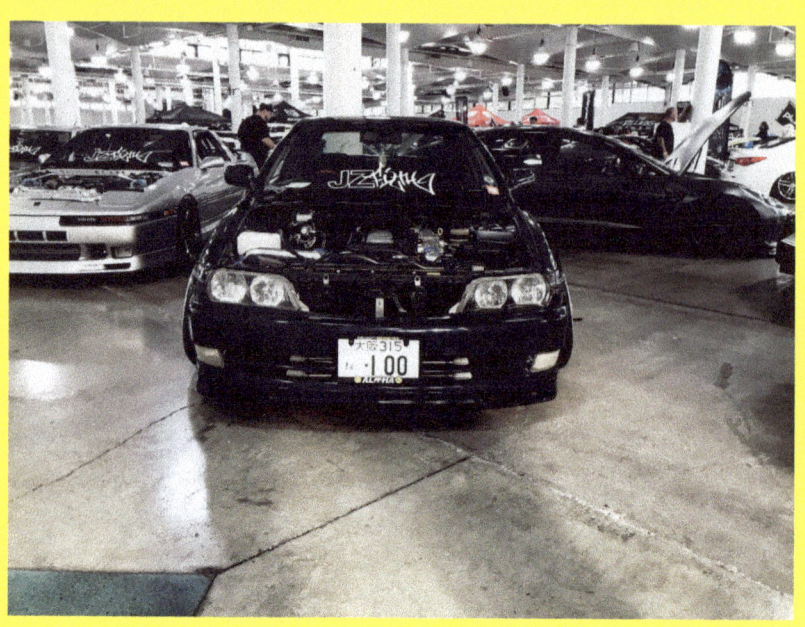

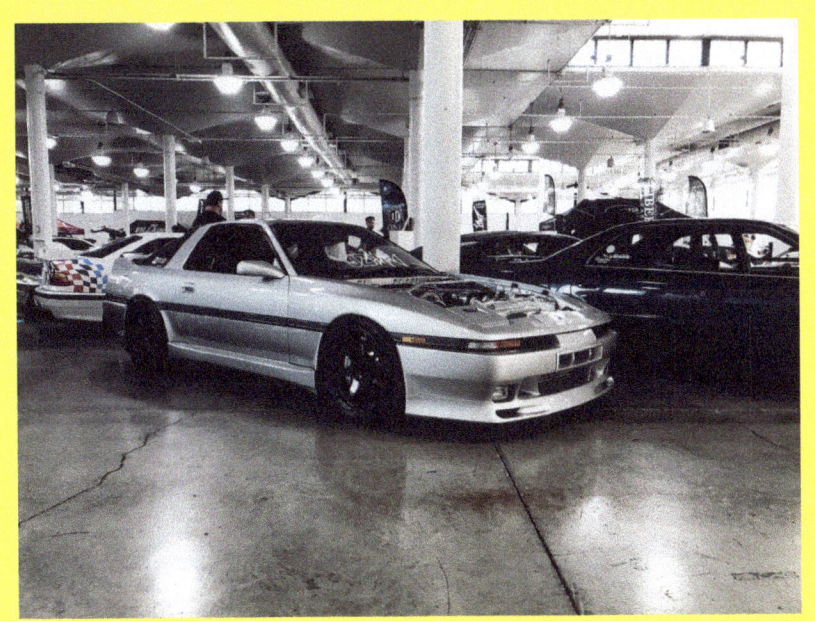

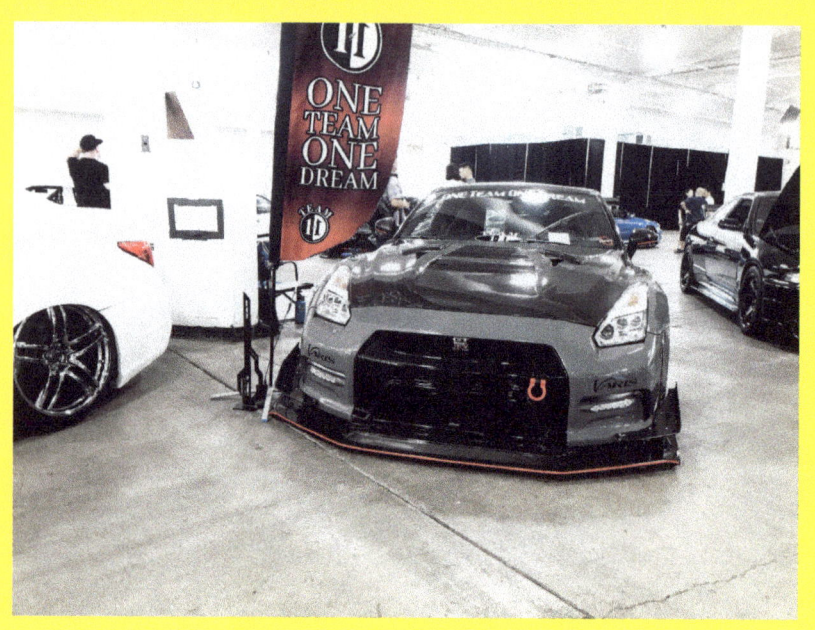

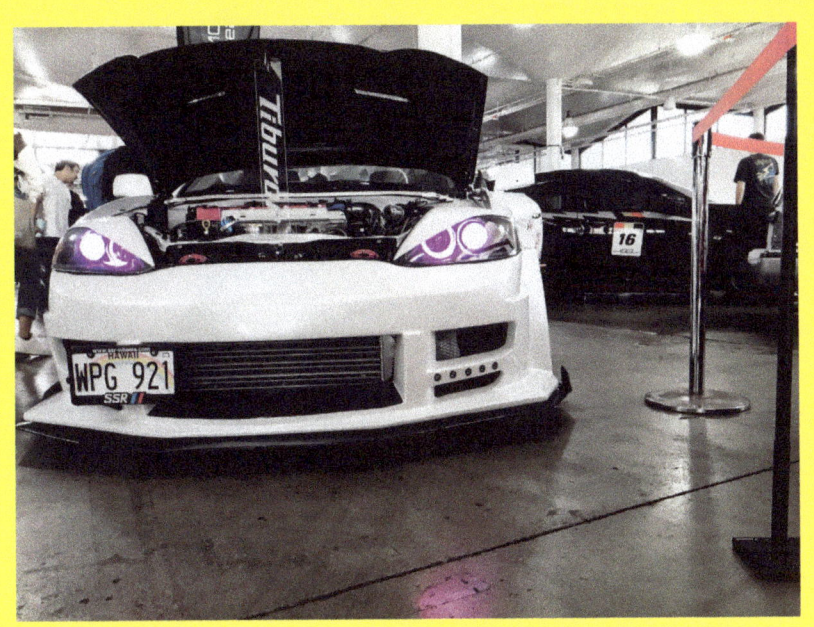

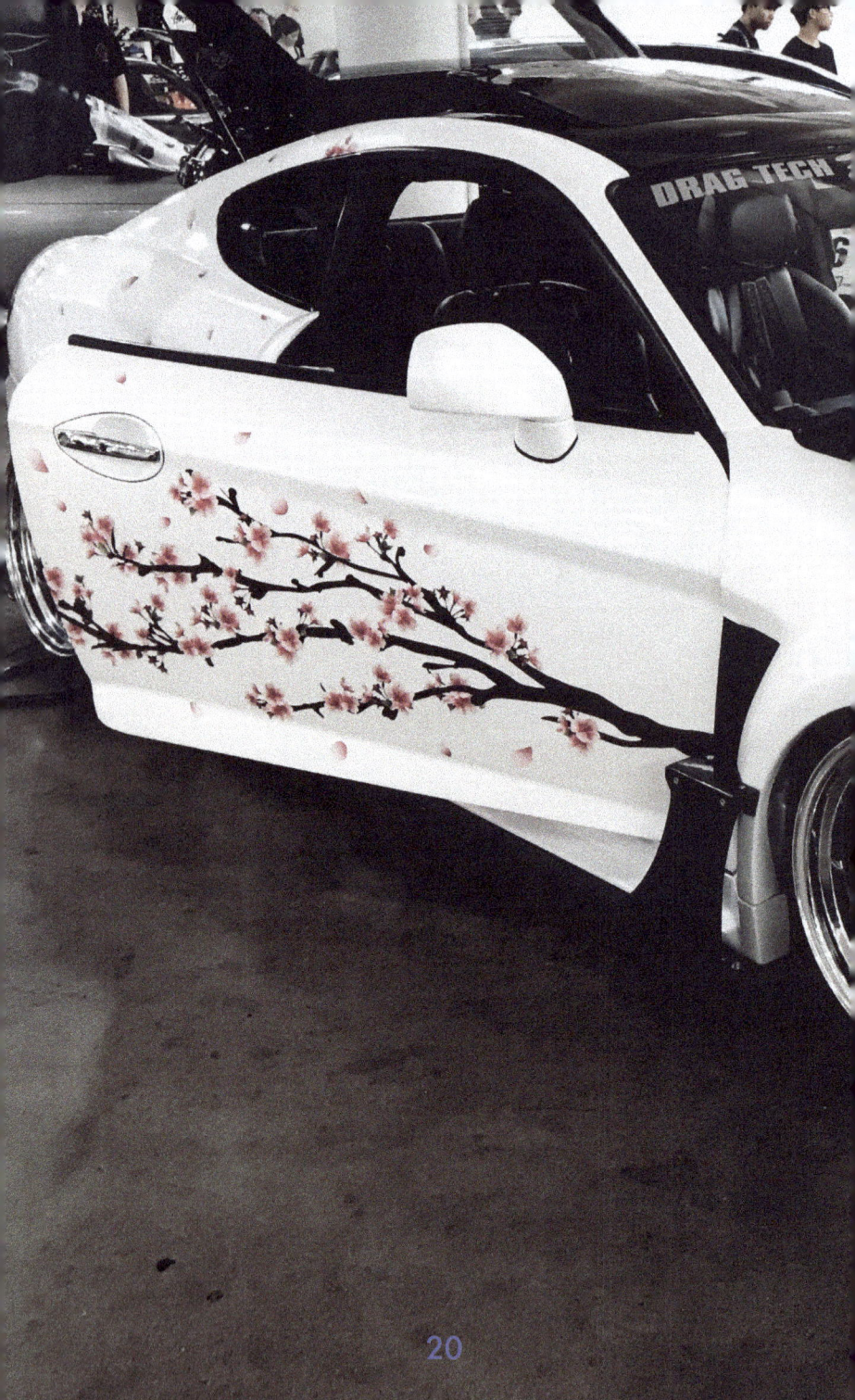

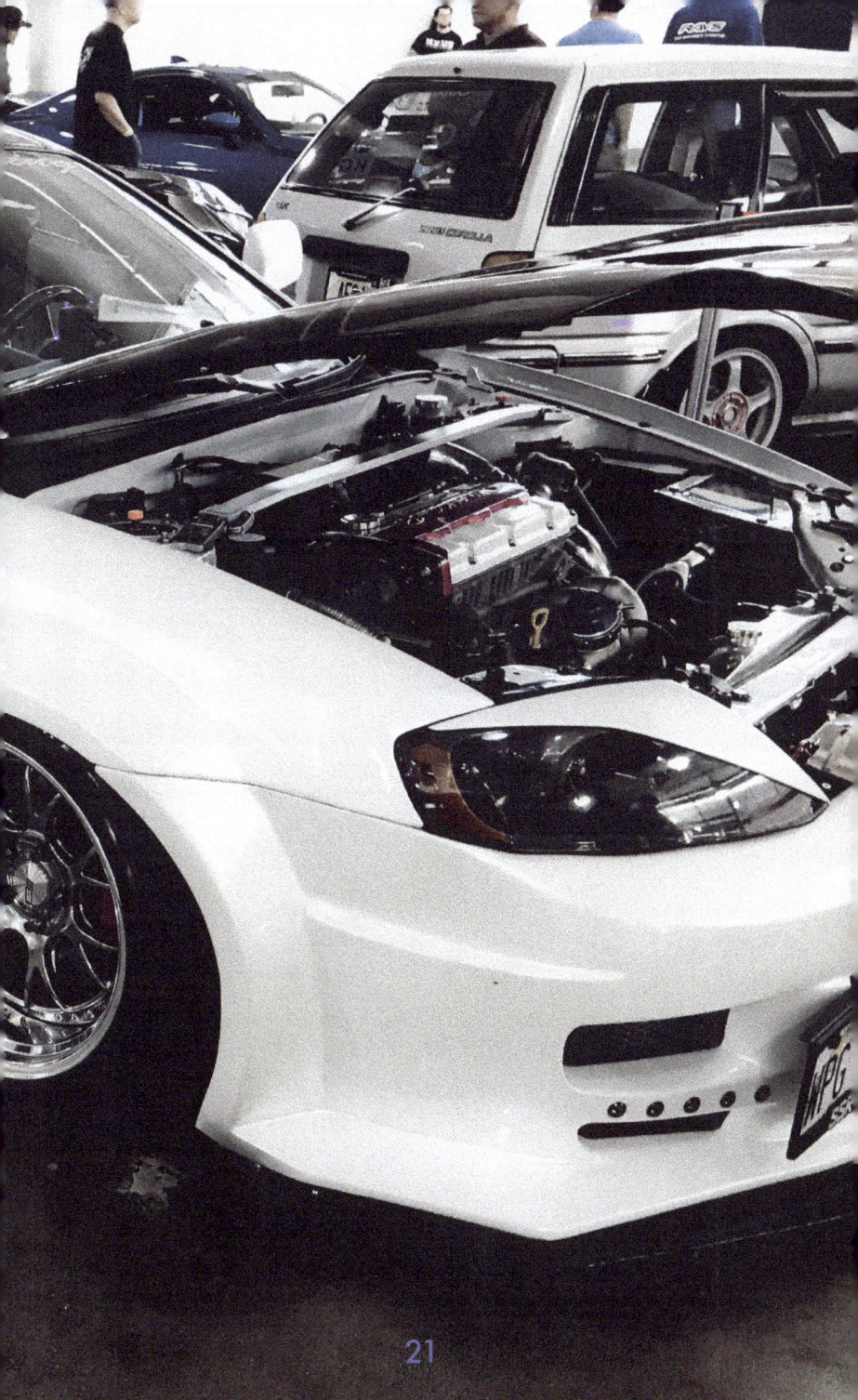

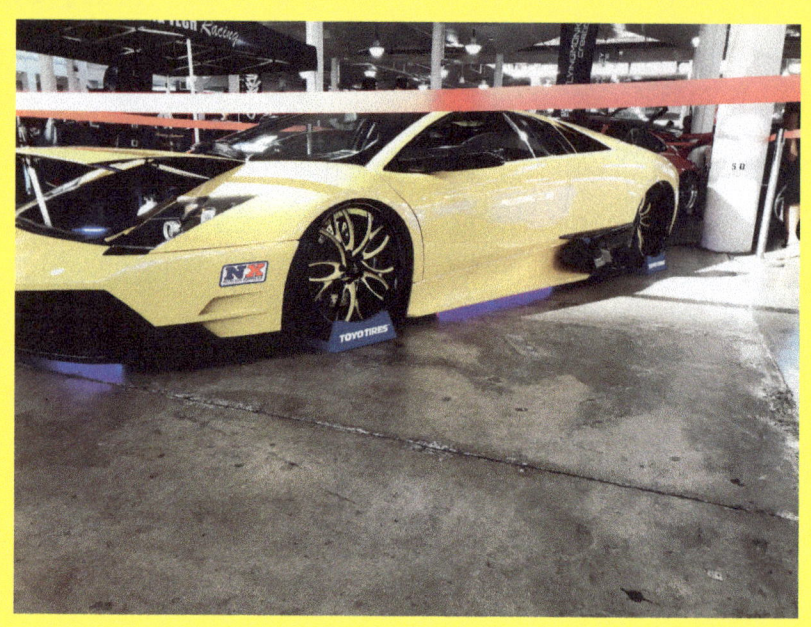

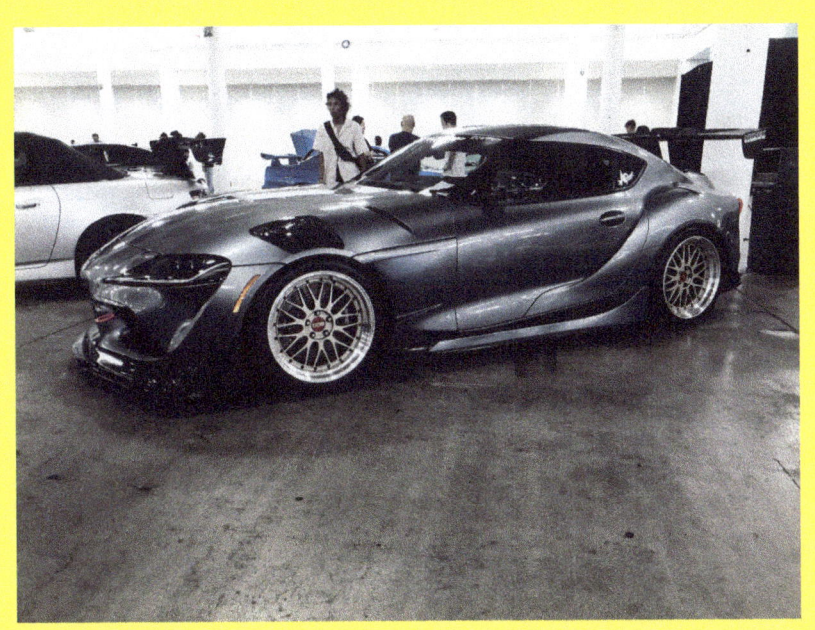

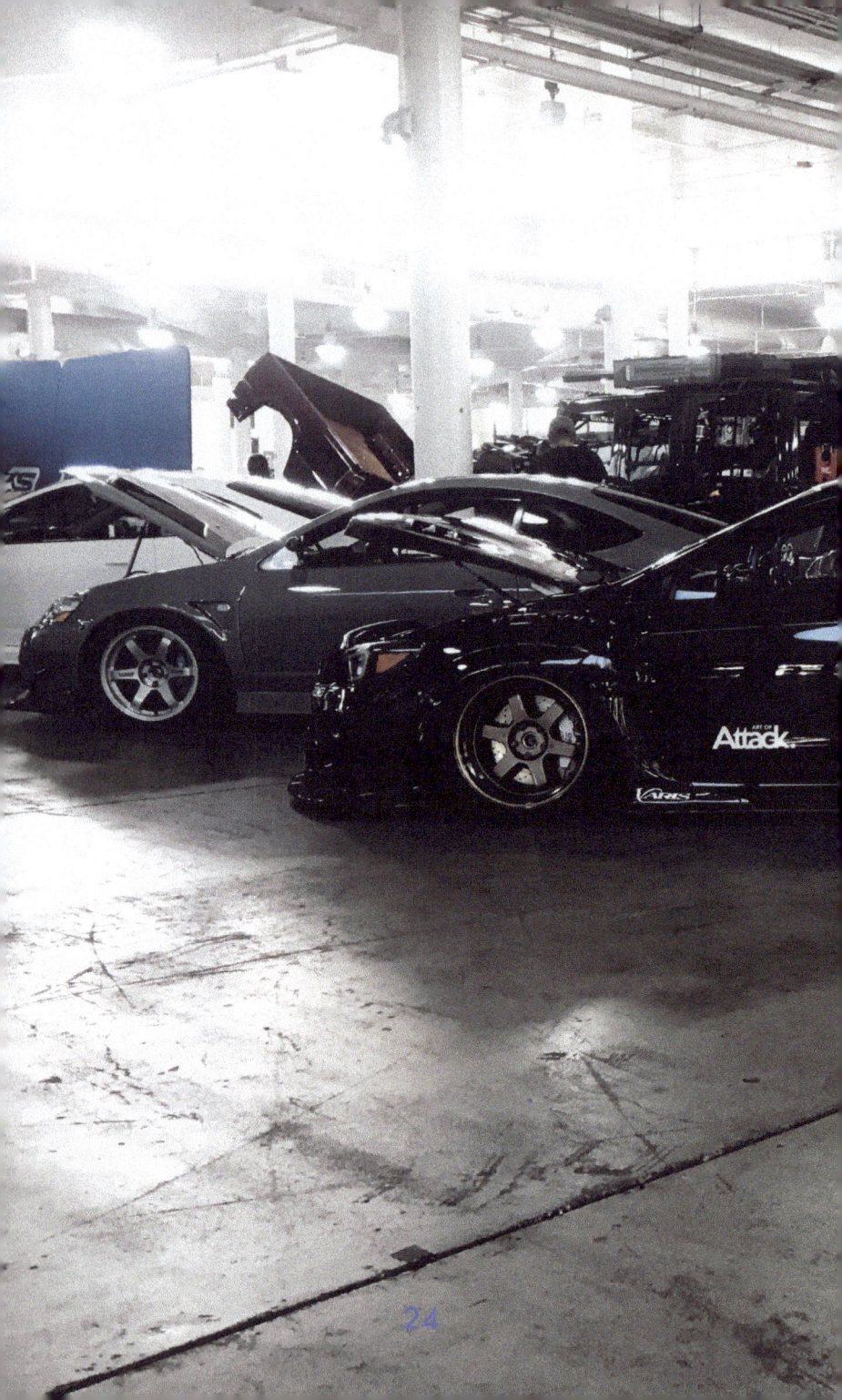

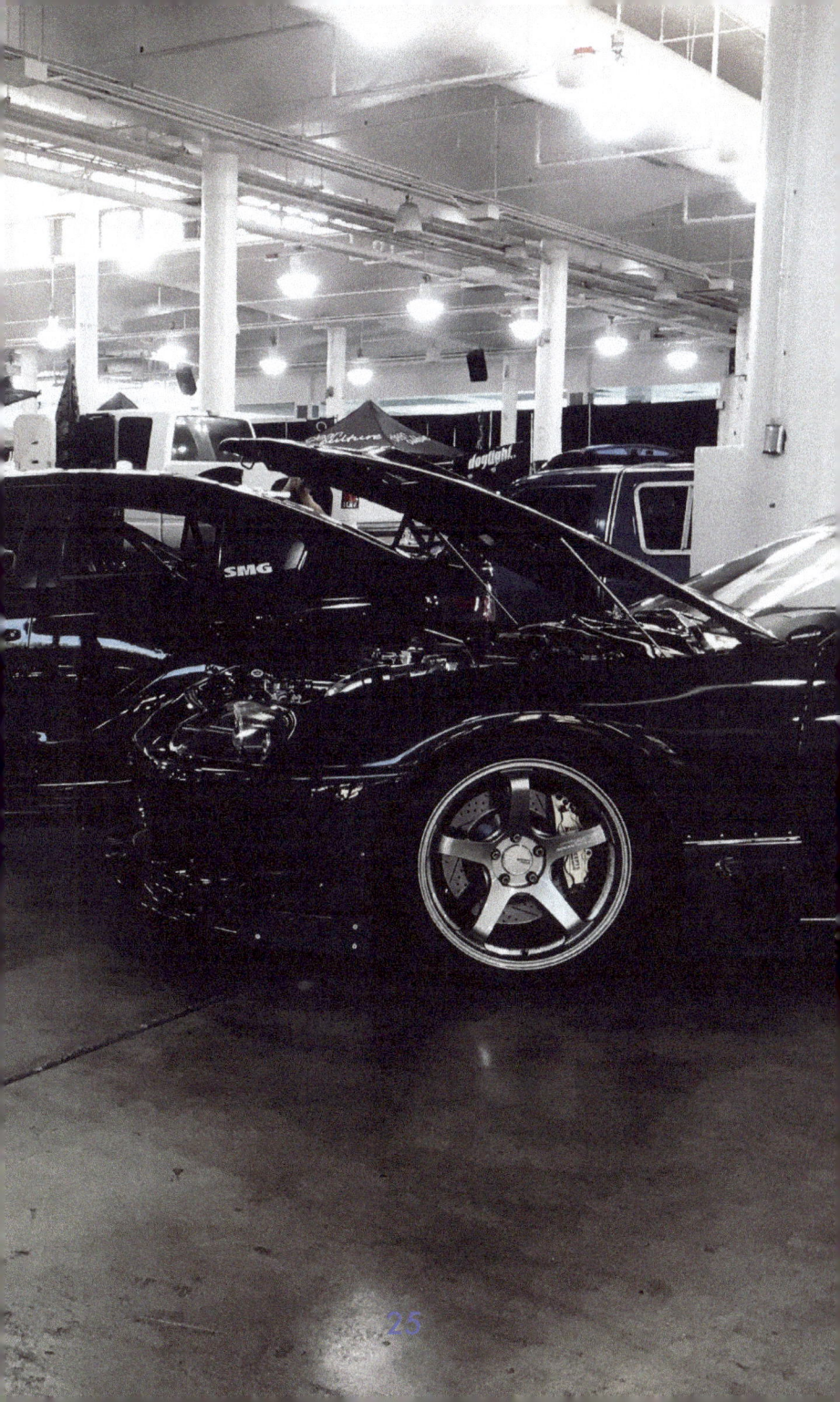

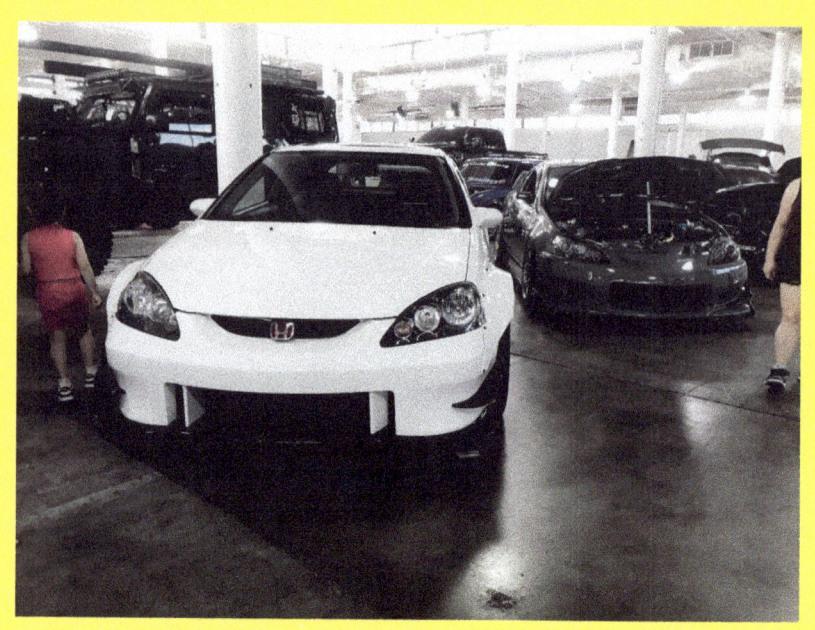

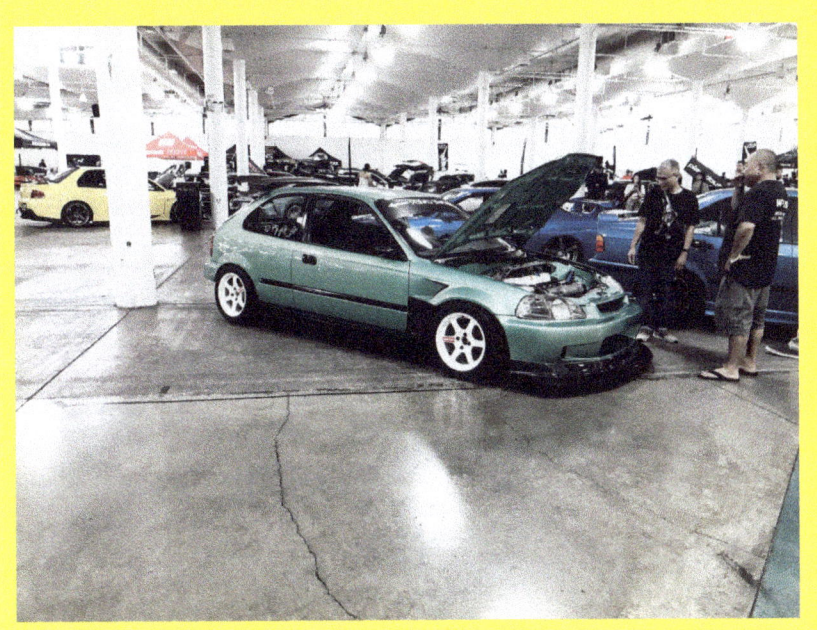

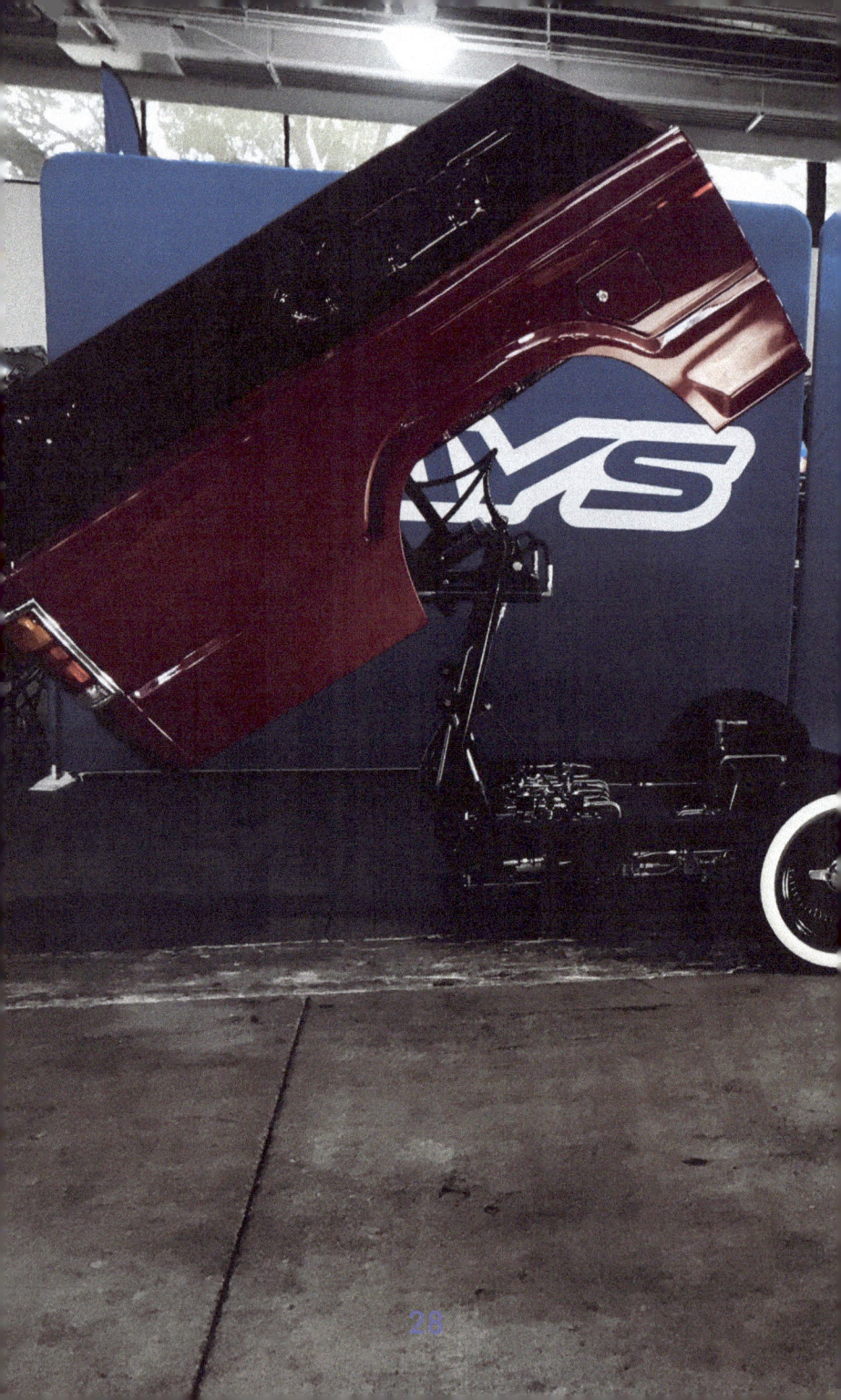

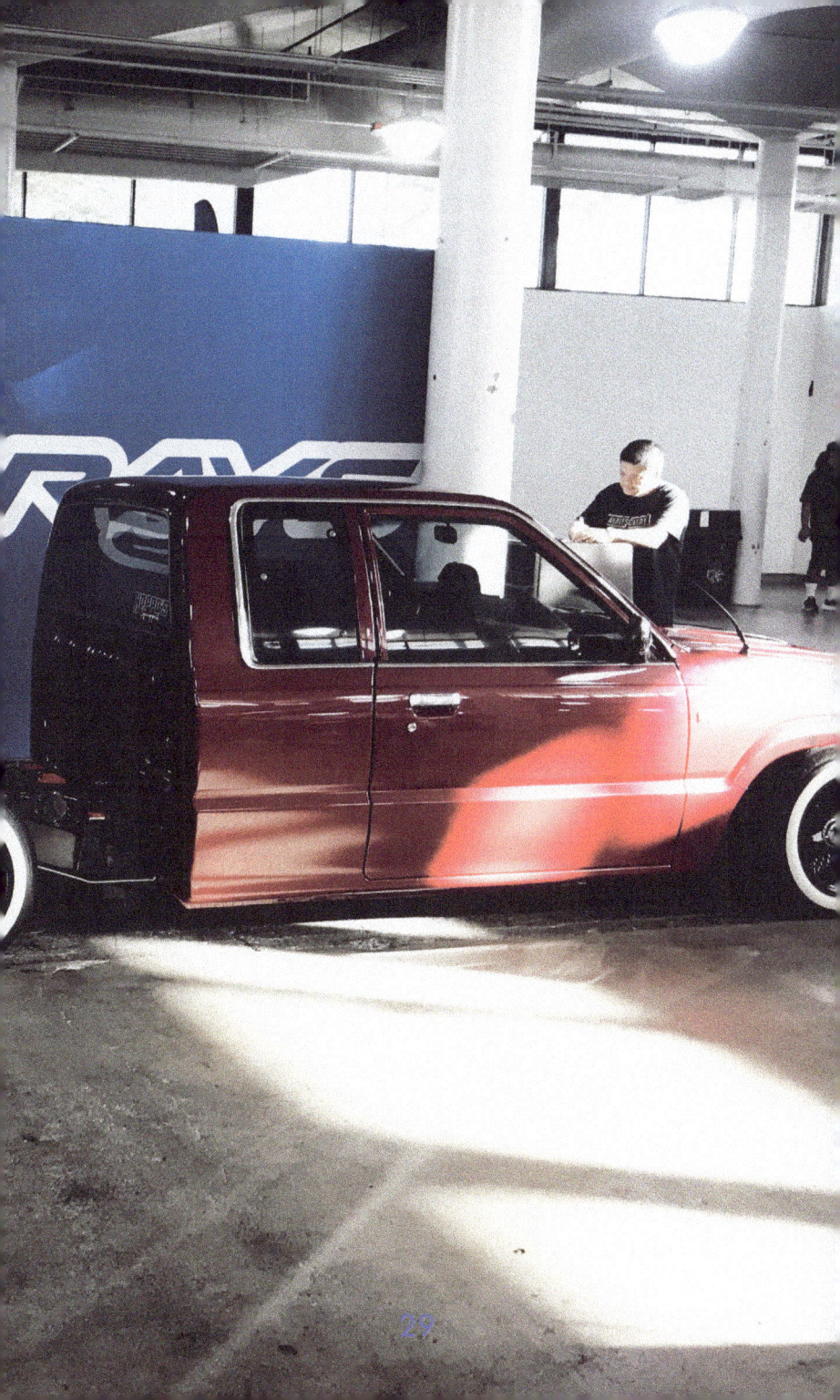

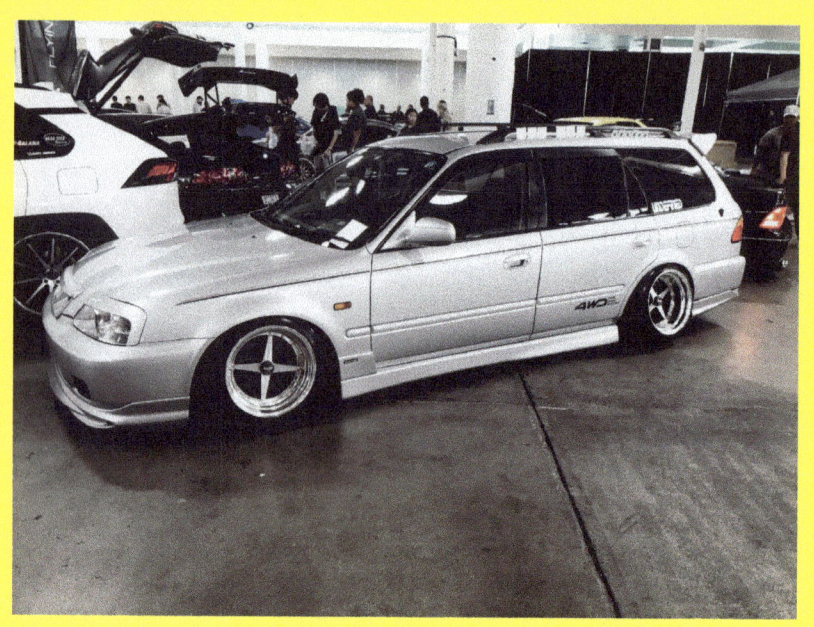

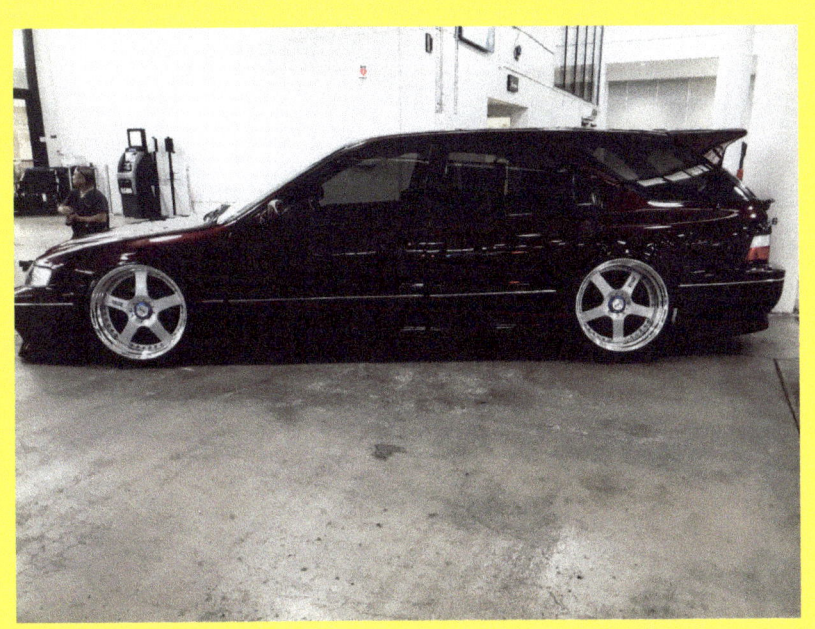

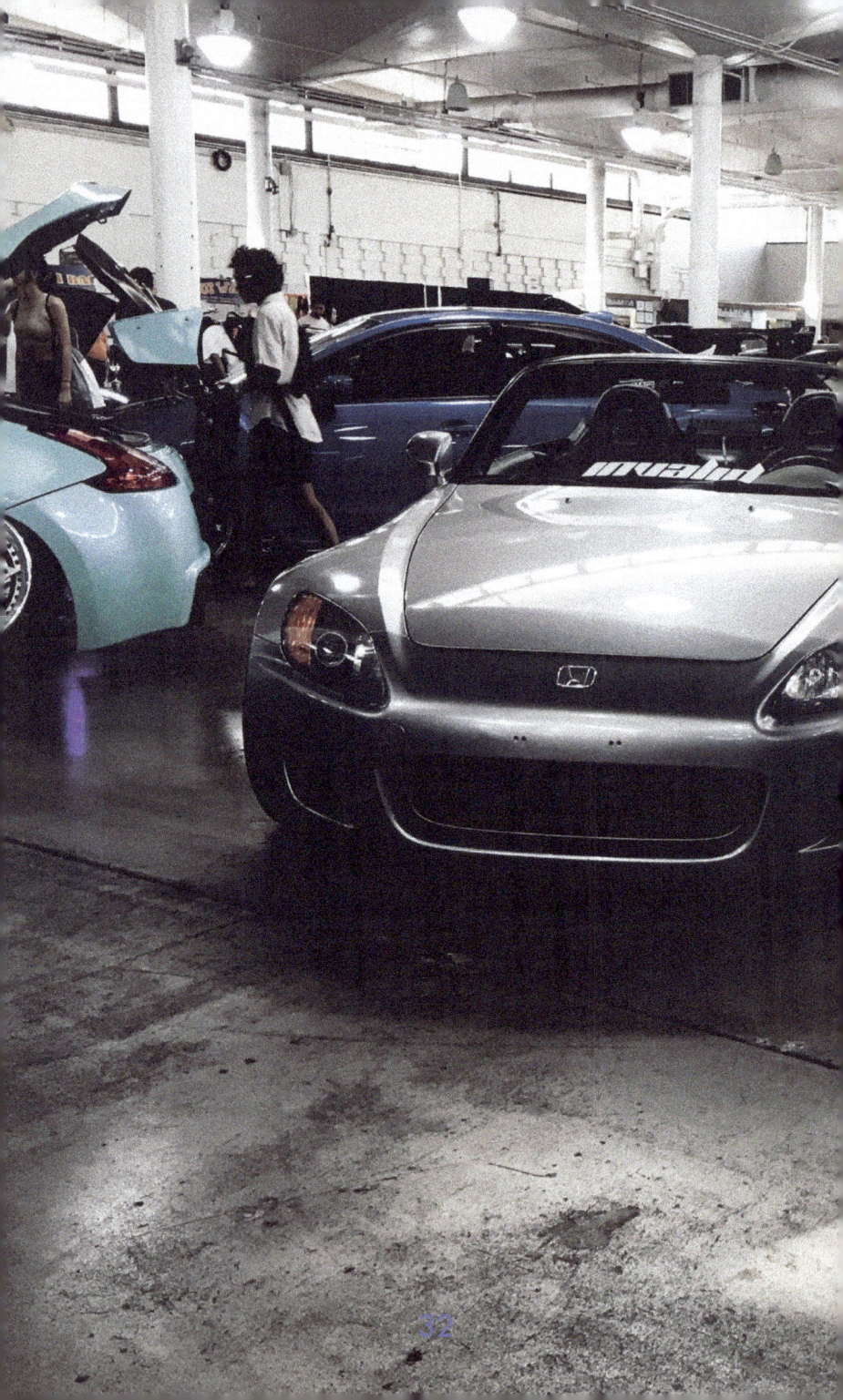

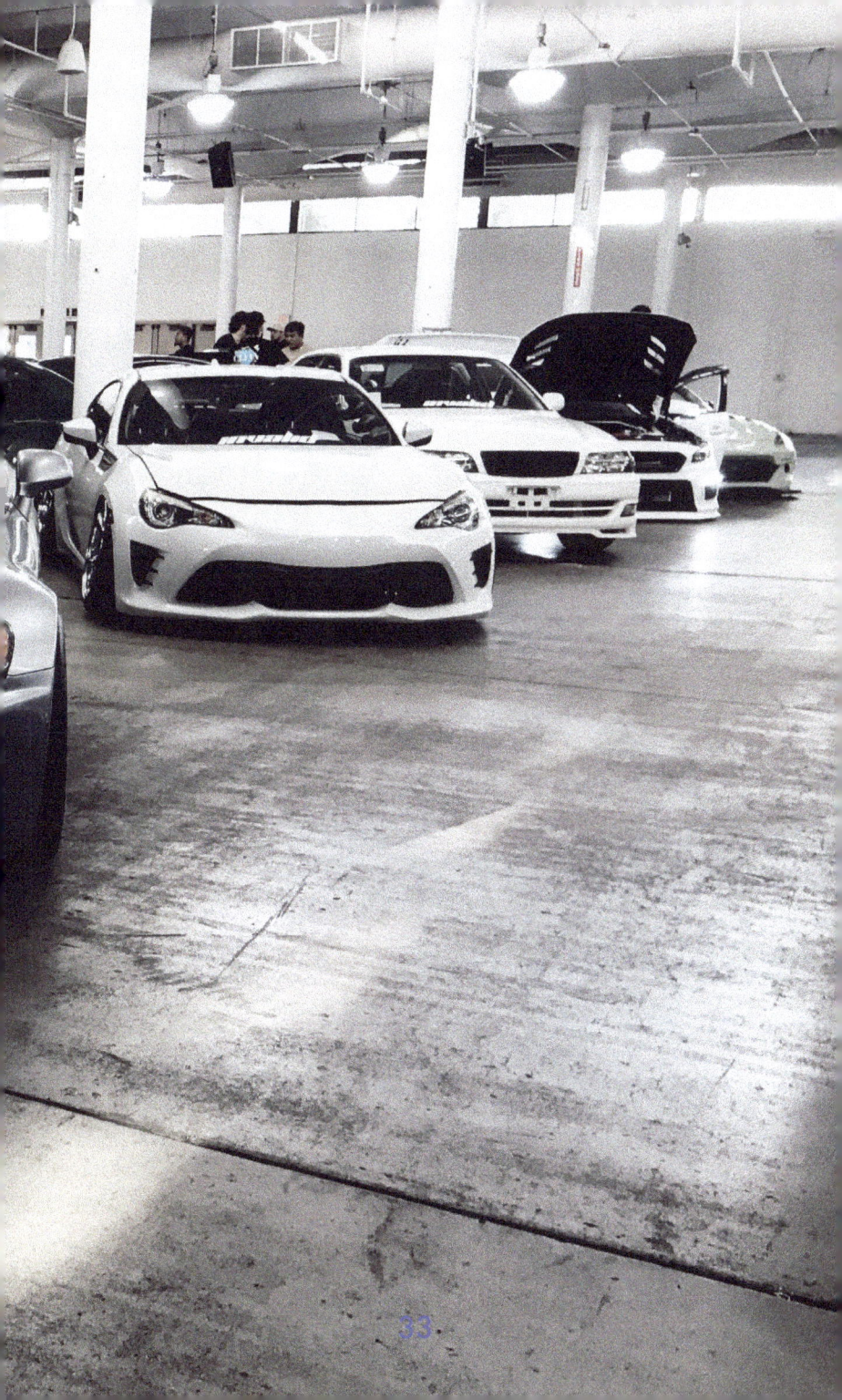

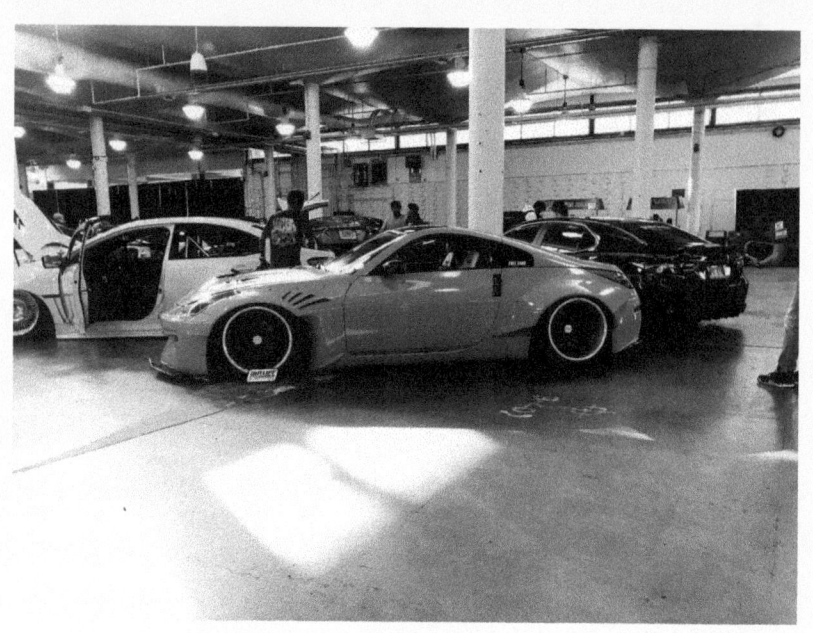

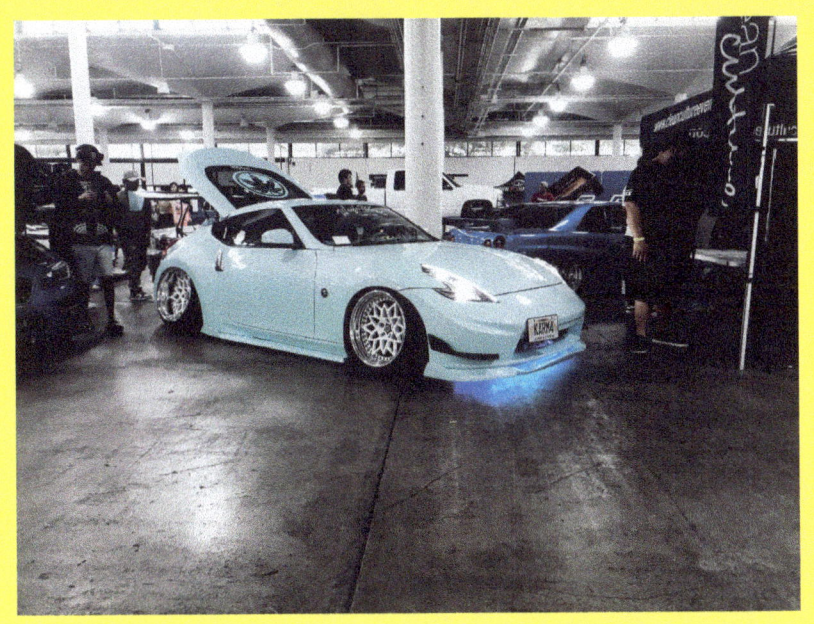

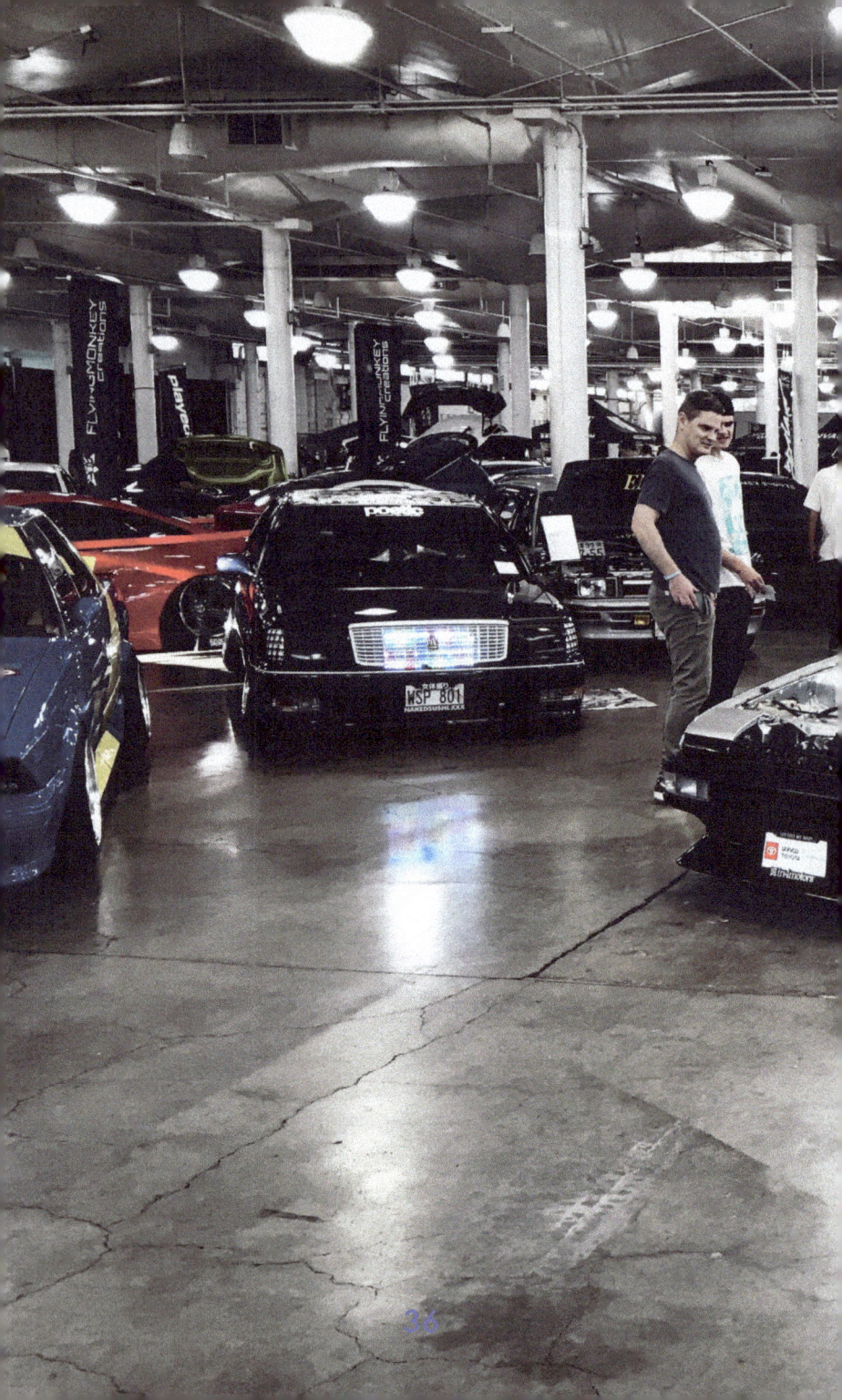

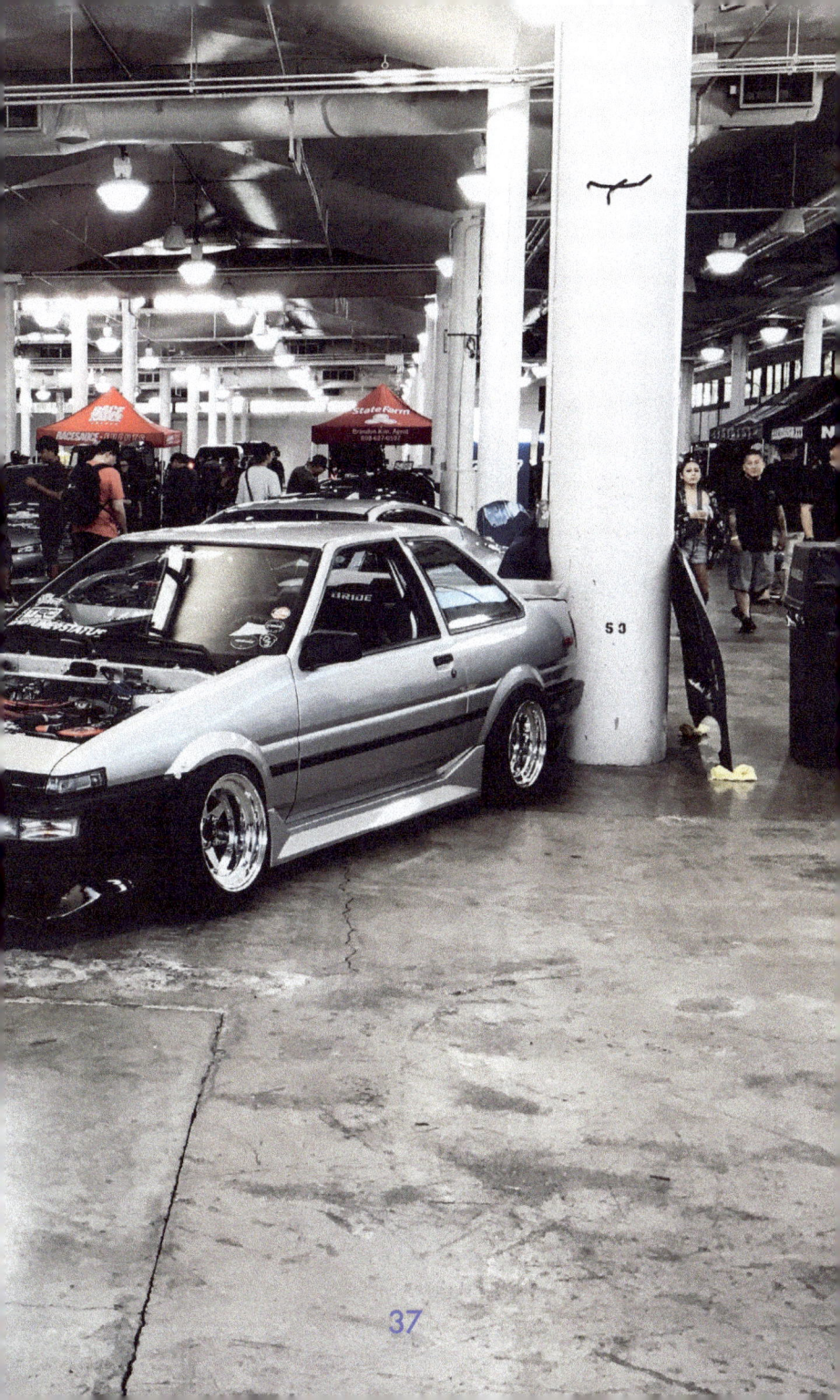

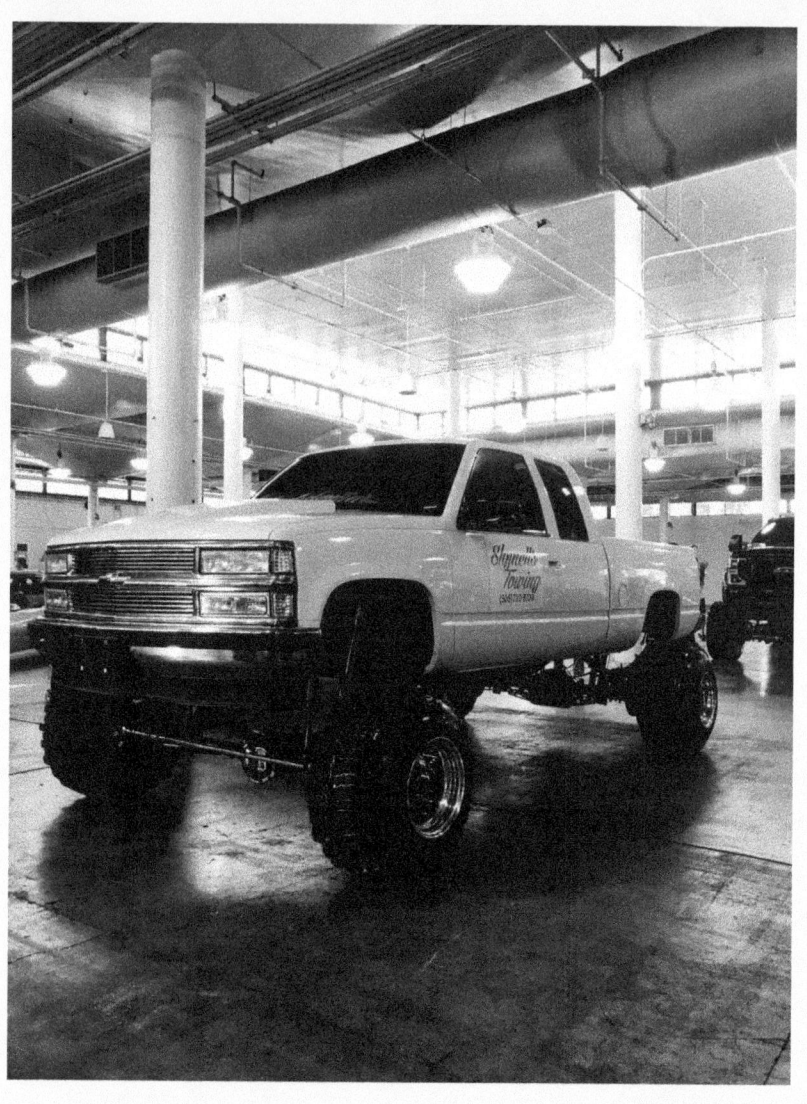

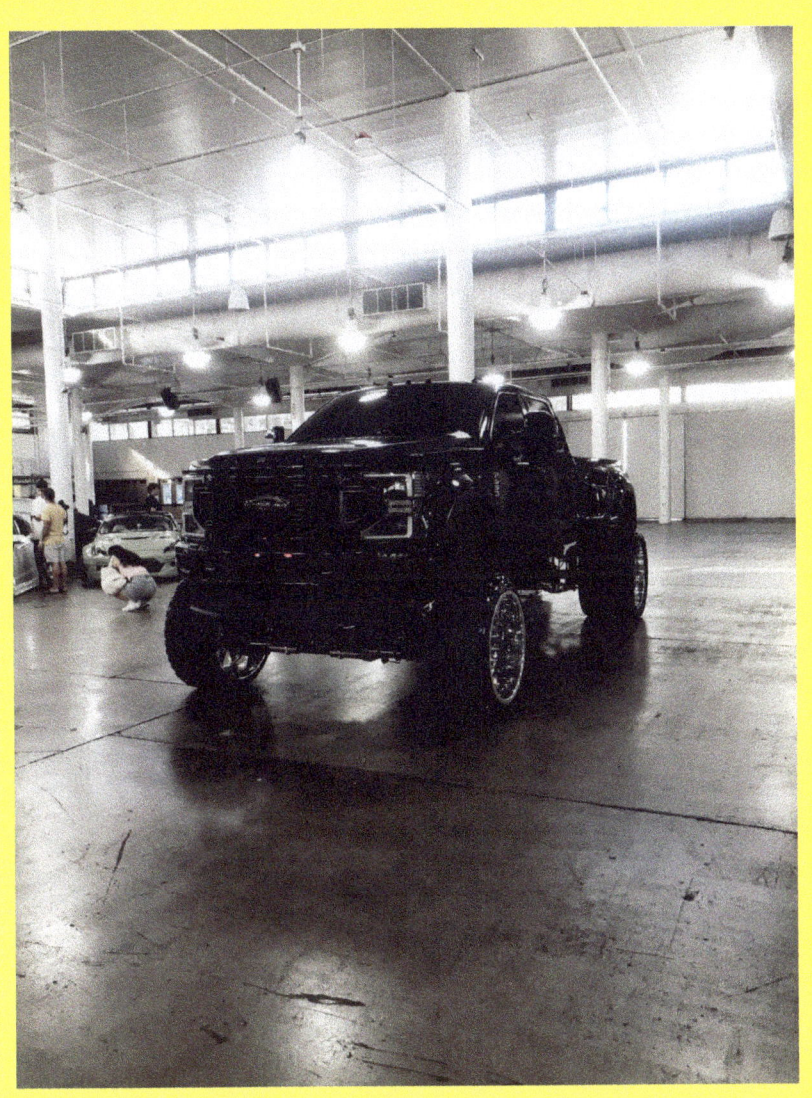

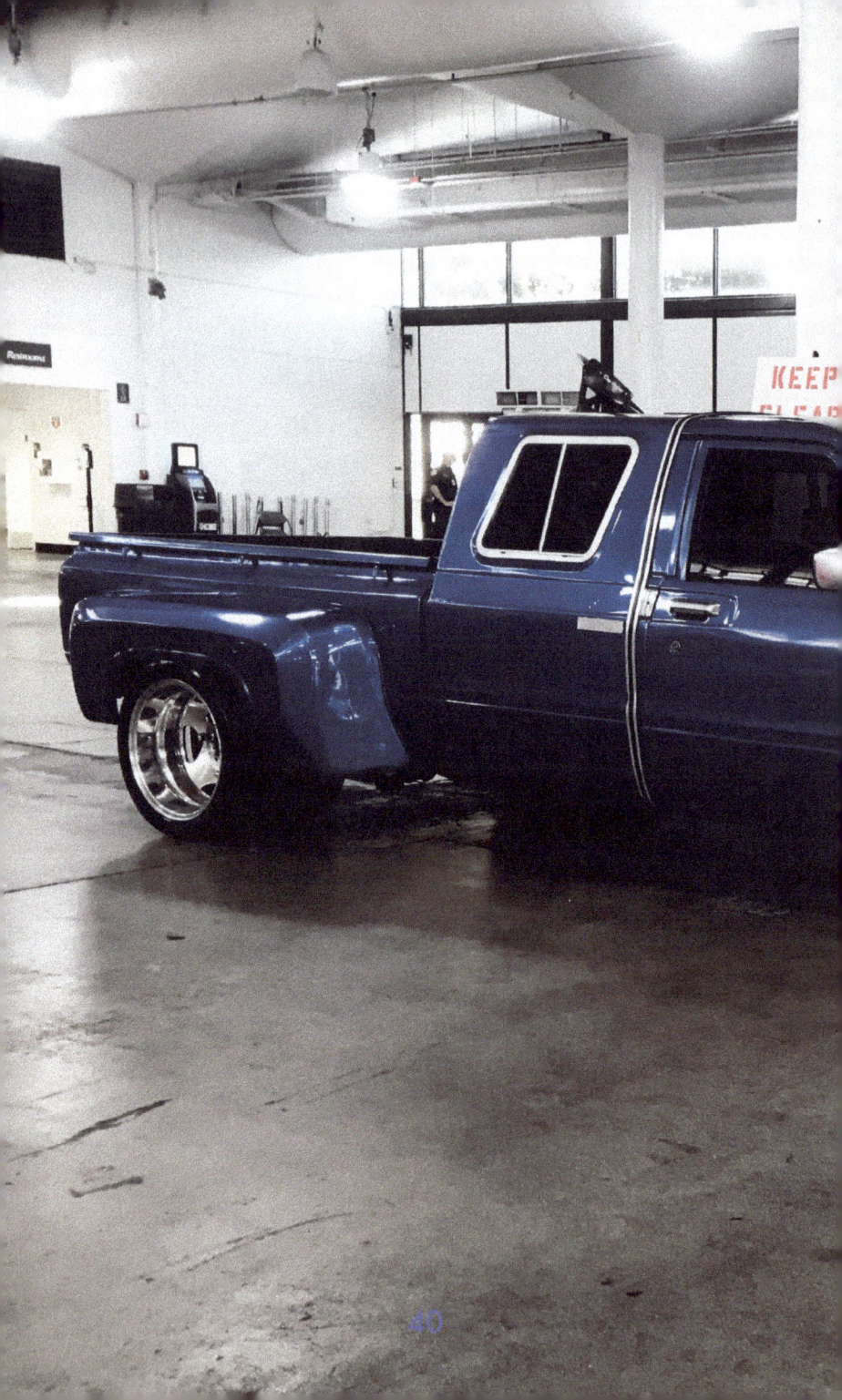

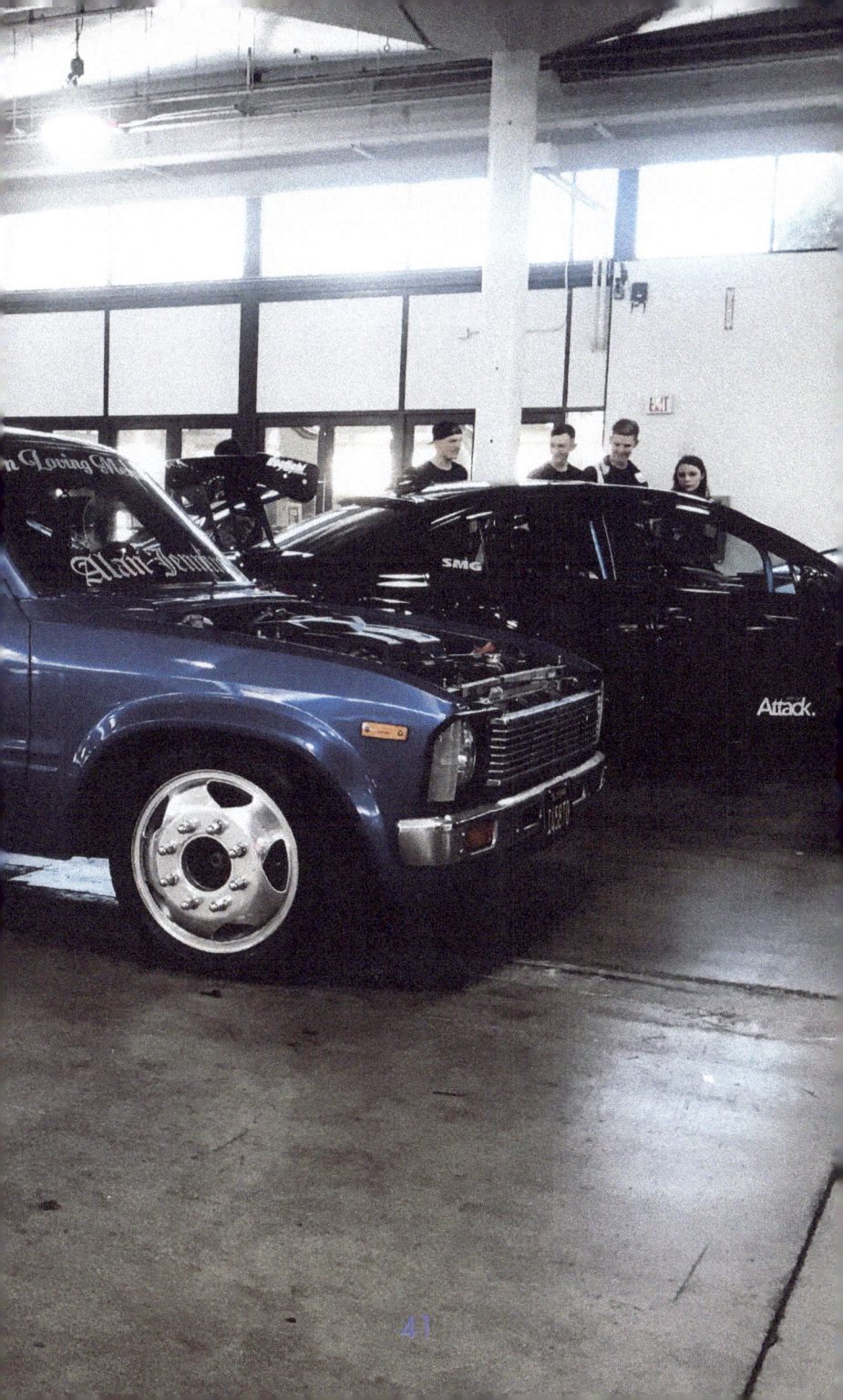

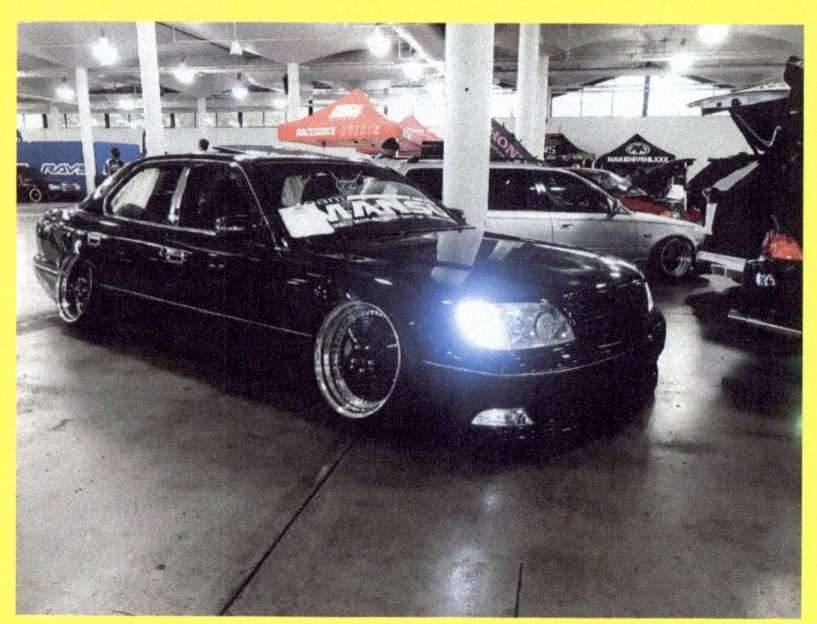

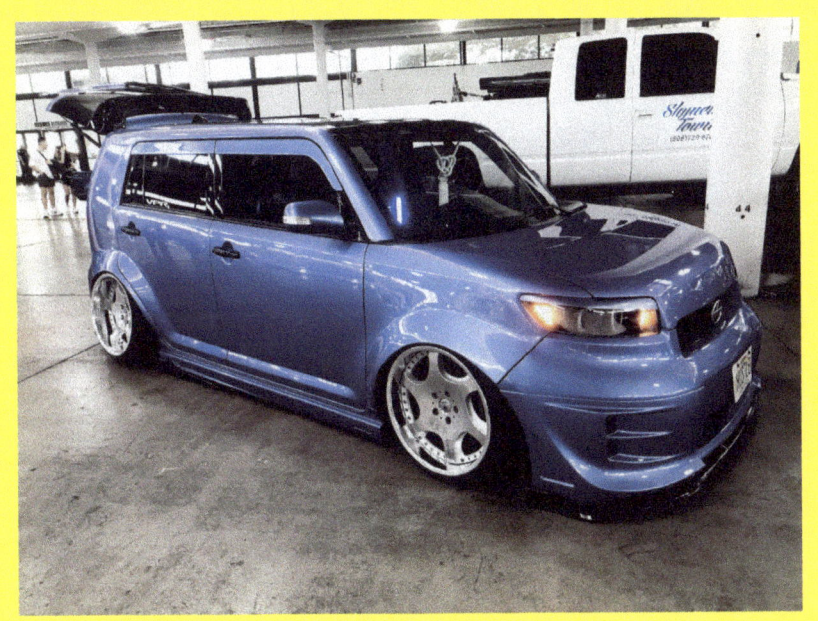

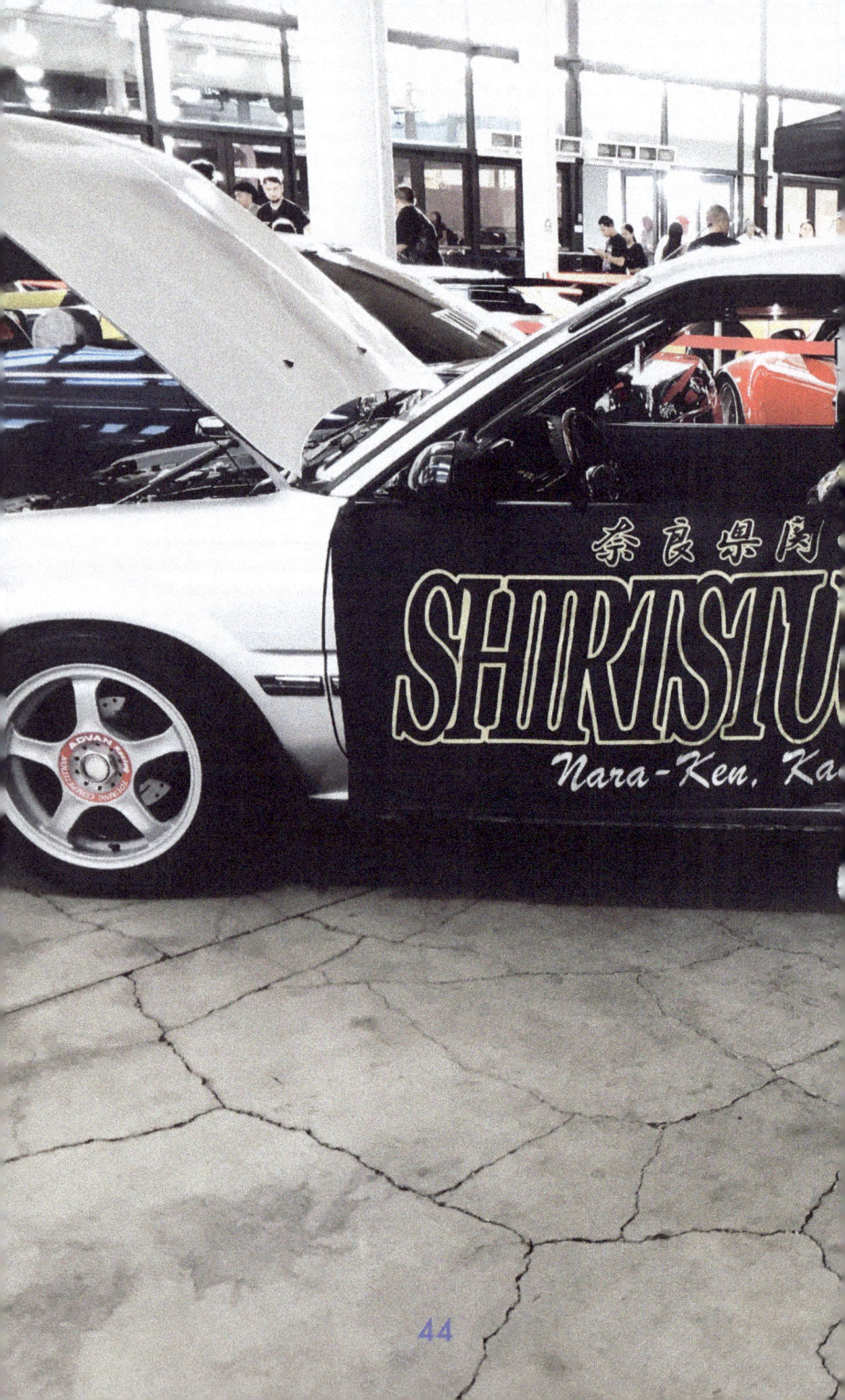

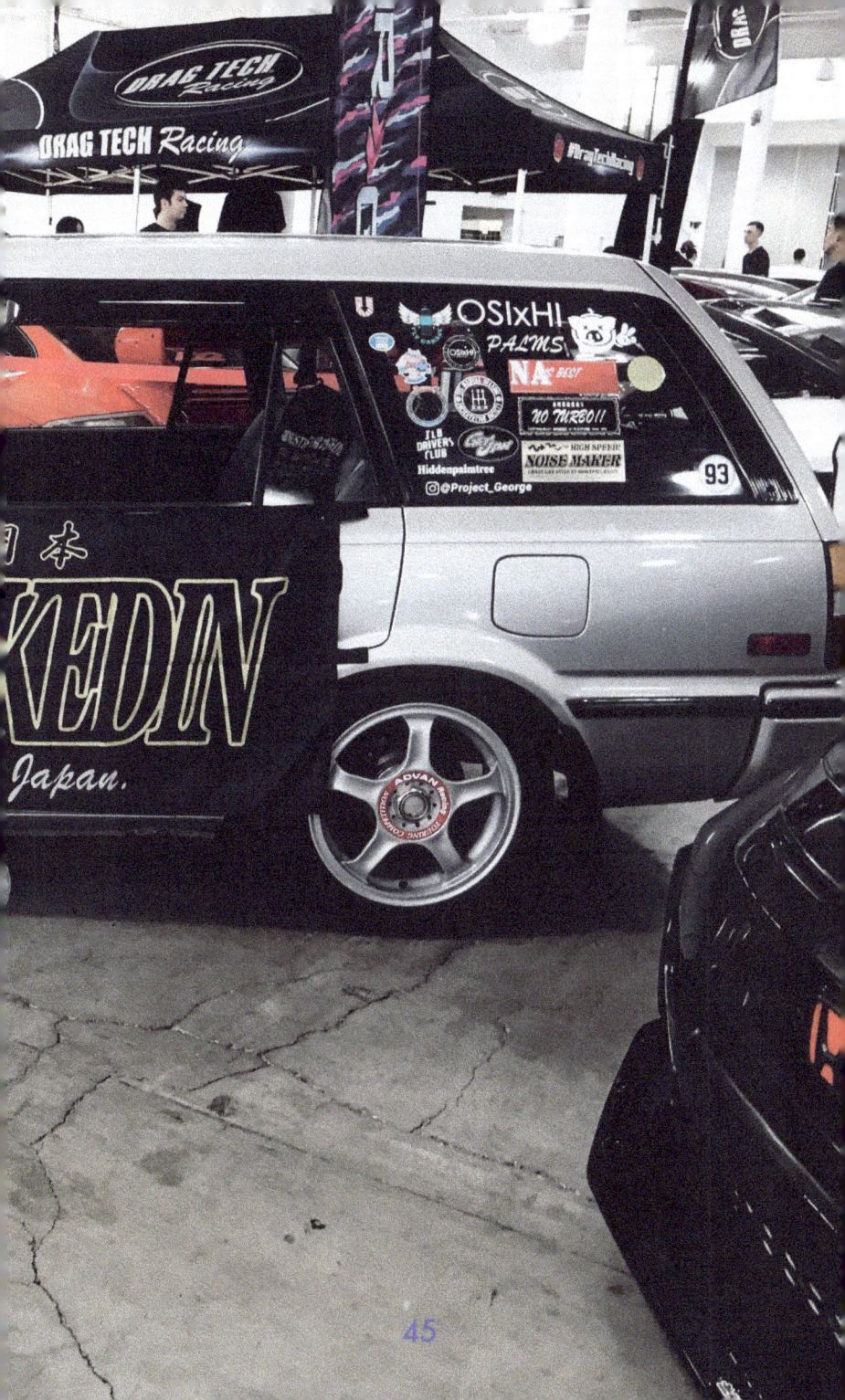

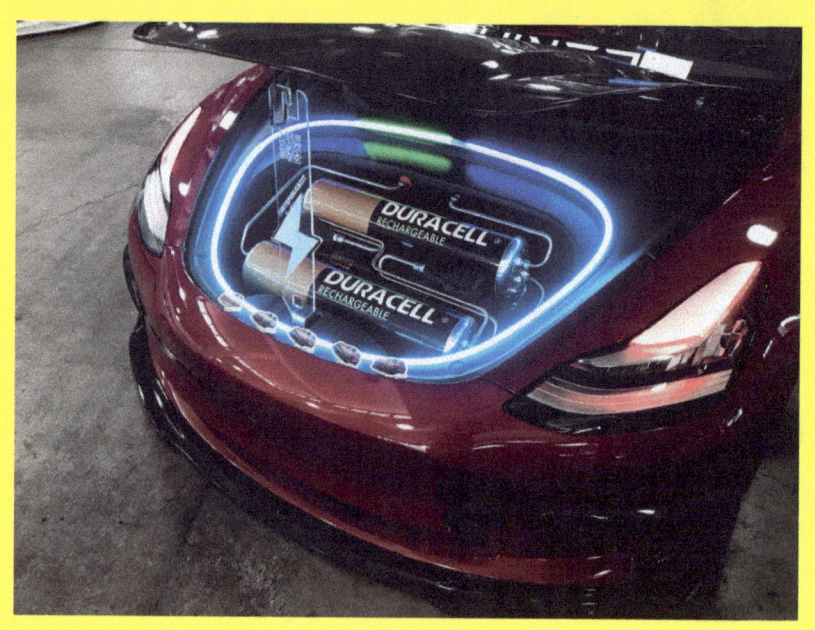

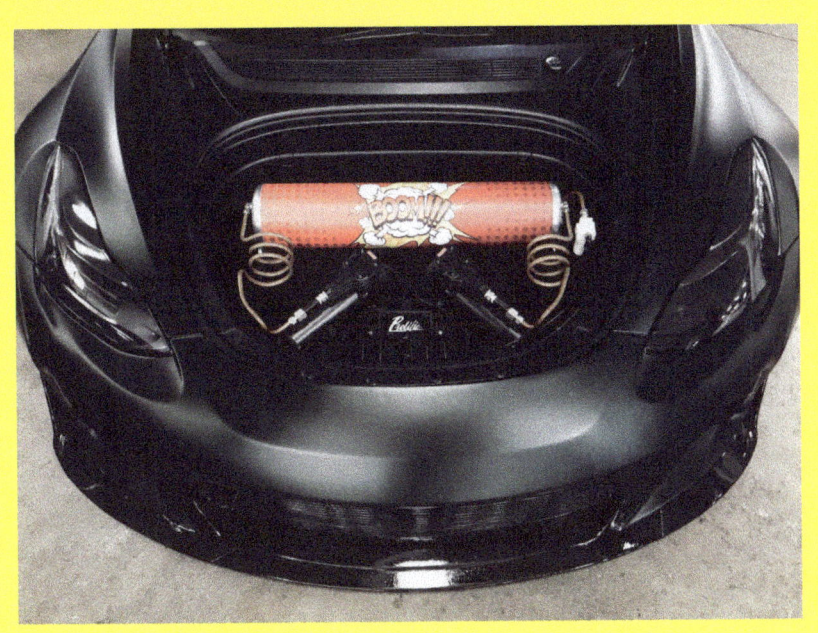

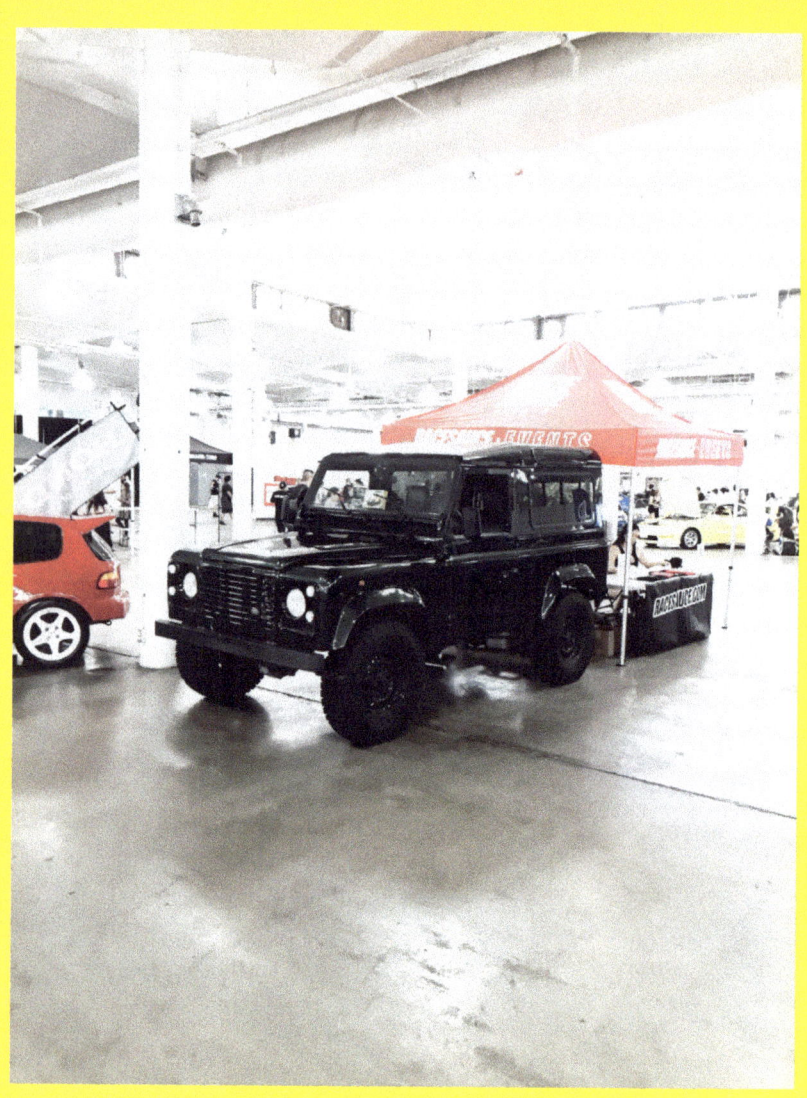

CAR SHOW

CAR SHOW

CAR SHOW

CAR SHOW

CAR SHOW

CAR SHOW

WEKFEST

WEKFEST

WEKFEST

WEKFEST

WEKFEST

WEKFEST

WEKFEST

WEKFEST

WEKFEST

WEKFEST

WEKFEST

WEKFEST

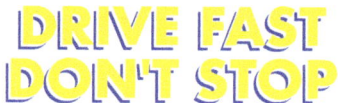

「 WWW.DRIVEFASTDONTSTOP.COM 」

PHOTOS BY
MATTHEW JOCELYN

♥